Marx Joyce Abbott Hardy Montaigne Machiavelli Chesterton Cooper Emerson Austen Defoe Melville Haggard Hugo Christie Carroll Eliot Grimm Stoker Molière Wilde Maupassant Byron Schiller Engels Garnett Einstein Fitzgerald Smith Hawthorne Kafka Goethe Dostoyevsky Cotton Hall Baum Kipling Doyle Willis Leslie Dumas Henry Nietzsche Flaubert Turgenev Balzac Stockton Vatsyayana Crane Burroughs Verne Curtis Tocqueville Whitman Gogol Vinci Homer Widger Tolstoy Busch Darwin Thoreau Potter Freud Zola Twain Plato Scott Lawrence Kant Jowett Stevenson Dickens Andersen Burton Hesse Harte London Descartes Cervantes Poe Aristotle Wells Voltaire Hale James Hastings Cooke Bunner Shakespeare Richter Chambers Irving Chekhov da Doré Swift Dante Shaw Wodehouse Benedict Alcott Pushkin Newton tredition®

tredition was established in 2006 by Sandra Latusseck and Soenke Schulz. Based in Hamburg, Germany, tredition offers publishing solutions to authors and publishing houses, combined with worldwide distribution of printed and digital book content. tredition is uniquely positioned to enable authors and publishing houses to create books on their own terms and without conventional manufacturing risks.

For more information please visit: www.tredition.com

TREDITION CLASSICS

This book is part of the TREDITION CLASSICS series. The creators of this series are united by passion for literature and driven by the intention of making all public domain books available in printed format again - worldwide. Most TREDITION CLASSICS titles have been out of print and off the bookstore shelves for decades. At tredition we believe that a great book never goes out of style and that its value is eternal. Several mostly non-profit literature projects provide content to tredition. To support their good work, tredition donates a portion of the proceeds from each sold copy. As a reader of a TREDITION CLASSICS book, you support our mission to save many of the amazing works of world literature from oblivion. See all available books at www.tredition.com.

Project Gutenberg

The content for this book has been graciously provided by Project Gutenberg. Project Gutenberg is a non-profit organization founded by Michael Hart in 1971 at the University of Illinois. The mission of Project Gutenberg is simple: To encourage the creation and distribution of eBooks. Project Gutenberg is the first and largest collection of public domain eBooks.

The Story of "Mormonism"

James Edward Talmage

Imprint

This book is part of TREDITION CLASSICS

Author: James Edward Talmage
Cover design: Buchgut, Berlin – Germany

Publisher: tredition GmbH, Hamburg - Germany
ISBN: 978-3-8424-5926-7

www.tredition.com
www.tredition.de

The intention of the TREDITION CLASSICS series is to make world literature in the public domain available in printed format. Literary enthusiasts and organizations, such as Project Gutenberg, worldwide have scanned and digitally edited the original texts. tredition has subsequently formatted and redesigned the content into a modern reading layout. Therefore, we cannot guarantee the exact reproduction of the original format of a particular historic edition. Please also note that no modifications have been made to the spelling, therefore it may differ from the orthography used today.

PREFACE

The Story of "Mormonism" as presented in the following pages is a revised and reconstructed version of lectures delivered by Dr. James E. Talmage at the University of Michigan, Cornell University, and elsewhere. The "Story" first appeared in print as a lecture report in the *Improvement Era,* and was afterward issued as a booklet from the office of the *Millennial Star,* Liverpool. In 1910 it was issued in a revised form by the Bureau of Information at Salt Lake City, in which edition the lecture style of direct address was changed to the ordinary form of essay. The present or third American edition has been revised and amplified by the author.

The "Story" has been translated and published abroad. Already versions have appeared in Swedish, modern Greek, and Russian.

The subject matter of *The Philosophy of "Mormonism"* was first presented as a lecture delivered by Dr. Talmage before the Philosophical Society of Denver. It appeared later in the columns of the *Improvement Era,* and translations have been published in pamphlet form in the Danish and German languages.

The present publication of these two productions is made in response to a steady demand.

THE PUBLISHERS.

Salt Lake City, Utah,
March, 1914.

THE STORY OF "MORMONISM"

CHAPTER I

In the minds of many, perhaps of the majority of people, the scene of the "Mormon" drama is laid almost entirely in Utah; indeed, the terms "Mormon question" and "Utah question" have been often used interchangeably. True it is, that the development of "Mormonism" is closely associated with the history of the long-time Territory and present State of Utah; but the origin of the system must be sought in regions far distant from the present gathering-place of the Latter-day Saints, and at a period antedating the acquisition of Utah as a part of our national domain.

The term "origin" is here used in its commonest application—that of the first stages apparent to ordinary observation—the visible birth of the system. But a long, long period of preparation had led to this physical coming forth of the "Mormon" religion, a period marked by a multitude of historical events, some of them preceding by centuries the earthly beginning of this modern system of prophetic trust. The "Mormon" people regard the establishment of their Church as the culmination of a great series of notable events. To them it is the result of causes unnumbered that have operated through ages of human history, and they see in it the cause of many developments yet to appear. This to them establishes an intimate relationship between the events of their own history and the prophecies of ancient times.

In reading the earliest pages of "Mormon" history, we are introduced to a man whose name will ever be prominent in the story of the Church—the founder of the organization by common usage of the term, the head of the system as an earthly establishment—one who is accepted by the Church as an ambassador specially commissioned of God to be the first revelator of the latter-day dispensation. This man is Joseph Smith, commonly known as the "Mormon" prophet. Rarely indeed does history present an organization, religious, social, or political, in which an individual holds as conspicuous and in all ways as important a place as does this man in the development of "Mormonism." The earnest investigator, the sincere truth-seeker, can ignore neither the man nor his work; for the Church under consideration has risen from the testimony solemnly set forth and the startling declarations made by this person, who, at the time of his earliest announcements, was a farmer's boy in the first half of his teens. If his claims to ordination under the hands of divinely commissioned messengers be fallacious, forming as they form the foundation of the Church organization, the superstructure cannot stand; if, on the other hand, such declarations be true, there is little cause to wonder at the phenomenally rapid rise and the surprising stability of the edifice so begun.

Joseph Smith was born at Sharon, Vermont, in December, 1805. He was the son of industrious parents, who possessed strong religious tendencies and tolerant natures. For generations his ancestors had been laborers, by occupation tillers of the soil; and though comfortable circumstances had generally been their lot, reverses and losses in the father's house had brought the family to poverty; so that from his earliest days the lad Joseph was made acquainted with the pleasures and pains of hard work. He is described as having been more than ordinarily studious for his years; and when that powerful wave of religious agitation and sectarian revival which characterized the first quarter of the last century, reached the home of the Smiths, Joseph with others of the family was profoundly affected. The household became somewhat divided on the subject of religion, and some of the members identified themselves with the more popular sects; but Joseph, while favorably impressed by the Methodists in comparison with others, confesses that his mind was sorely troubled over the contemplation of the strife and tumult existing among the religious bodies; and he hesitated. He tried in vain to solve the mystery presented to him in the warring factions of what professed to be the Church of Christ. Surely, thought he, these several churches, opposed as they are to one another on what appear to be the vital points of religion, cannot all be right. While puzzling over this anomaly he chanced upon this verse in the epistle of St. James:

> "If any of you lack wisdom, let him ask of God, that giveth to all men liberally, and upbraideth not; and it shall be given him."

In common with so many others, the earnest youth found here within the scriptures, admonition and counsel as directly applicable to his case and circumstances as if the lines had been addressed to him by name. A brief period of hesitation, in which he shrank from the thought that a mortal like himself, weak, youthful, and unlearned, should approach the Creator with a personal request, was followed by a humble and contrite resolution to act upon the counsel of the ancient apostle. The result, to which he bore solemn record (testifying at first with the simplicity and enthusiasm of youth, afterward confirming the declaration with manhood's increasing powers, and at last voluntarily sealing the testimony with his life's blood,) proved most startling to the sectarian world—a world in which according to popular belief no new revelation of truth was possible. It is a surprising fact that while growth, progress, advancement, development of known truths and the acquisition of new ones, characterize every living science, the sectarian world has declared that nothing new must be expected as direct revelation from God.

The testimony of this lad is, that in response to his supplication, drawn forth by the admonition of an inspired apostle, he received a divine ministration; heavenly beings manifested themselves to him—two, clothed in purity, and alike in form and feature. Pointing to the other, one said, "This is my beloved Son, hear Him." In answer to the lad's prayer, the heavenly personage so designated informed Joseph that the Spirit of God dwelt not with warring sects, which, while professing a form of godliness, denied the power thereof, and that he should join none of them. Overjoyed at the glorious manifestation thus granted unto him, the boy prophet could not withhold from relatives and acquaintances tidings of the heavenly vision. From the ministers, who had been so energetic in their efforts to convert the boy, he received, to his surprise, abuse and ridicule. "Visions and manifestations from God," said they, "are of the past, and all such things ceased with the apostles of old; the canon of scripture is full; religion has reached its perfection in plan, and, unlike all other systems contrived or accepted by human kind, is incapable of development or growth. It is true God lives, but He cares not for His children of modern times as He did for those of ancient days; He has shut Himself away from the people, closed the windows of heaven, and has suspended all direct communication with the people of earth."

The persecution thus originating with those who called themselves ministers of the gospel of Christ spread throughout the community; and the sects that before could not agree together nor abide in peace, became as one in their efforts to oppose the youth who thus testified of facts, which though vehemently denounced, produced an effect that alarmed them the more. And such a spectacle has ofttimes presented itself before the world—men who cannot tolerate one another in peace swear fidelity and mutual support in strife with a common opponent. The importance of this alleged revelation from the heavens to the earth is such as to demand attentive consideration. If a fact, it is a full contradiction of the vague theories that had been increasing and accumulating for centuries, denying personality and parts to Deity.

In 1820, there lived one person who knew that the word of the Creator, "Let us make man in our own image, after our likeness," had a meaning more than in metaphor. Joseph Smith, the youthful prophet and revelator of the nineteenth century, knew that the Eternal Father and the well-beloved Son, Jesus Christ, were in form and stature like unto perfect men; and that the human family was in very truth of divine origin. But this wonderful vision was not the only manifestation of heavenly power and personality made to the young man, nor the only incident of the kind destined to bring upon him the fury of persecution. Sometime after this visitation, which constituted him a living witness of God unto men, and which demonstrated the great fact that humanity is the child of Deity, he was visited by an immortal personage who announced himself as Moroni, a messenger sent from the presence of God. The celestial visitor stated that through Joseph as the earthly agent the Lord would accomplish a great work, and that the boy would come to be known by good and evil repute amongst all nations. The angel then announced that an ancient record, engraven on plates of gold, lay hidden in a hill near by, which record gave a history of the nations that had of old inhabited the American continent, and an account of the Savior's ministrations among them. He further explained that with the plates were two sacred stones, known as Urim and Thummim, by the use of which the Lord would bring forth a translation of the ancient record. Joseph further testifies that he was told that if he remained faithful to his trust and the confidence reposed in him, he would some day receive the record into his keeping, and be commissioned and empowered to translate it. In due time these promises were literally fulfilled, and the modern version of these ancient writings was given to the world.

The record proved to be an account of certain colonies of immigrants to this hemisphere from the east, who came several centuries before the Christian era. The principal company was led by one Lehi, described as a personage of some importance and wealth, who had formerly lived at Jerusalem in the reign of Zedekiah, and who left his eastern home about 600 B.C. The book tells of the journeyings across the water in vessels constructed according to revealed plan, of the peoples' landing on the western shores of South America probably somewhere in Chile, of their prosperity and rapid growth amid the bounteous elements of the new world, of the increase of pride and consequent dissension accompanying the accumulation of material wealth, and of the division of the people into factions which became later two great nations at enmity with one another. One part following Nephi, the youngest and most gifted son of Lehi, designated themselves *Nephites*; the other faction, led by Laman, the elder and wicked brother of Nephi, were known as *Lamanites*.

The Nephites lived in cities, some of which attained great size and were distinguished by great architectural beauty. Continually advancing northward, these people in time occupied the greater part of the valleys of the Orinoco, the Amazon, and the Magdalena. During the thousand years covered by the Nephite record, the people crossed the Isthmus of Panama, which is graphically described as a neck of land but a day's journey from sea to sea, and successively occupied extensive tracts in what is now Mexico, the valley of the Mississippi, and the Eastern States. It is not to be supposed that these vast regions were all populated at any one time by the Nephites; the people were continually moving to escape the depredations of their hereditary foes, the Lamanites; and they abandoned in turn all their cities established along the course of migration. The unprejudiced student sees in the discoveries of the ancient and now forest-covered cities of Mexico, Central America, Yucatan, and the northern regions of South America, collateral testimony having a bearing upon this history.

Before their more powerful foes, the Nephites dwindled and fled; until about the year 400 A.D. they were entirely annihilated after a series of decisive battles, the last of which was fought near the very hill, called Cumorah, in the State of New York, where the hidden record was subsequently revealed to Joseph Smith.

The Lamanites led a roving, aggressive life; kept few or no records, and soon lost the art of history writing. They lived on the results of the chase and by plunder, degenerating in habit until they became typical progenitors of the dark-skinned race, afterward discovered by Columbus and named American Indians.

The last writer in the ancient record, and the one who hid away the plates in the hill Cumorah, was Moroni—the same personage who appeared as a resurrected being in the nineteenth century, a divinely appointed messenger sent to reveal the depository of the sacred documents; but the greater part of the plates since translated had been engraved by the father of Moroni, the Nephite prophet Mormon. This man, at once warrior, prophet and historian, had made a transcript and compilation of the heterogeneous records that had accumulated during the troubled history of the Nephite nation; this compilation was named on the plates "The Book of Mormon," which name has been given to the modern translation—a work that has already made its way over most of the civilized world. The translation and publication of the Book of Mormon were marked by many scenes of trouble and contention, but success attended the undertaking, and the first edition of the work appeared in print in 1830.

The question, "What is the Book of Mormon?"—a very pertinent one on the part of every earnest student and investigator of this phase of American history—has been partly answered already. The work has been derisively called the "Mormon Bible," a name that carries with it the misrepresentation that in the faith of this people the book takes the place of the scriptural volume which is universally accepted by Christian sects. No designation could be more misleading, and in every way more untruthful. The Latter-day Saints have but one "Bible" and that the Holy Bible of Christendom. They place it foremost amongst the standard works of the Church; they accept its admonitions and its doctrines, and accord thereto a literal significance; it is to them, and ever has been, the word of God, a compilation made by human agency of works by various inspired writers; they accept its teachings in fulness, modifying the meaning in no wise, except in the rare cases of undoubted mistranslation, concerning which Biblical scholars of all faiths differ and criticize; and even in such cases their reverence for the sacred letter renders them even more conservative than the majority of Bible commentators and critics in placing free construction upon the text. The historical part of the Jewish scriptures tells of the divine dealings with the people of the eastern hemisphere; the Book of Mormon recounts the mercies and judgments of God, the inspired teachings of His prophets, the rise and fall of His people as organized communities on the western continent.

The Latter-day Saints believe the coming forth of the Book of Mormon to have been foretold in the Bible, as its destiny is prophesied of within its own lids; it is to the people the true "stick of Ephraim" which Ezekiel declared should become one with the "stick of Judah"—or the Bible. The people challenge the most critical comparison between this record of the west and the Holy Scriptures of the east, feeling confident that no discrepancy exists in letter or spirit. As to the original characters in which the record was engraved, copies were shown to learned linguists of the day and pronounced by them as closely resembling the Reformed Egyptian writing.

Let us revert, however, to the facts of history concerning this new scripture, and the reception accorded the printed volume.

The Book of Mormon was before the world; the Church circulated the work as freely as possible. The true account of its origin was rejected by the general public, who thus, assumed the responsibility of explaining in some plausible way the source of the record. Among the many false theories propounded, perhaps the most famous is the so-called Spaulding story. Solomon Spaulding, a clergyman of Amity, Pennsylvania, died in 1816. He wrote a romance to which no name other than "Manuscript Story" was given, and which, but for the unauthorized use of the writer's name and the misrepresentation of his motives, would never have been published. Twenty years after the author's death, one Hurlburt, an apostate "Mormon," announced that he had recognized a resemblance between the "Manuscript Story" and the Book of Mormon, and expressed a belief that the work brought forward by Joseph Smith was nothing but the Spaulding romance revised and amplified. The apparent credibility of the statement was increased by various signed declarations to the effect that the two were alike, though no extracts for comparison were presented. But the "Manuscript Story" was lost for a time, and in the absence of proof to the contrary, reports of the parallelism between the two works multiplied. By a fortunate circumstance, in 1884, President James H. Fairchild, of Oberlin College, and a literary friend of his—a Mr. Rice—while examining a heterogeneous collection of old papers which had been purchased by the gentleman last named, found the original manuscript of the "Story."

After a careful perusal and comparison with the Book of Mormon, President Fairchild declared in an article published in the New York *Observer*, February 5, 1885:

> The theory of the origin of the Book of Mormon in the traditional manuscript of Solomon Spaulding will probably have to be relinquished. * * * Mr. Rice, myself, and others compared it [the Spaulding manuscript] with the Book of Mormon and could detect no resemblance between the two, in general or in detail. There seems to be no name nor incident common to the two. The solemn style of the Book of Mormon in imitation of the English scriptures does not appear in the manuscript. * * * Some other explanation of the origin of the Book of Mormon must be found if any explanation is required.

The manuscript was deposited in the library of Oberlin College where it now reposes. Still, the theory of the "Manuscript Found," as

Spaulding's story has come to be known, is occasionally pressed into service in the cause of anti-"Mormon" zeal, by some whom we will charitably believe to be ignorant of the facts set forth by President Fairchild. A letter of more recent date, written by that honorable gentleman in reply to an inquiring correspondent, was published in the *Millennial Star*, Liverpool, November 3, 1898, and is as follows:

OBERLIN COLLEGE, OHIO,
October 17, 1895.

J. R. HINDLEY, ESQ.,

Dear Sir: We have in our college library an original manuscript of Solomon Spaulding—unquestionably genuine.

I found it in 1884 in the hands of Hon. L. L. Rice, of Honolulu, Hawaiian Islands. He was formerly state printer at Columbus, Ohio, and before that, publisher of a paper in Painesville, whose preceding publisher had visited Mrs. Spaulding and obtained the manuscript from her. It had lain among his old papers forty years or more, and was brought out by my asking him to look up anti-slavery documents among his papers.

The manuscript has upon it the signatures of several men of Conneaught, Ohio, who had heard Spaulding read it and knew it to be his. No one can see it and question its genuineness. The manuscript has been printed twice, at least;—once by the Mormons of Salt Lake City, and once by the Josephite Mormons of Iowa. The Utah Mormons obtained the copy of Mr. Rice, at Honolulu, and the Josephites got it of me after it came into my possession.

This manuscript is not the original of the Book of Mormon.

Yours very truly,
JAMES H. FAIRCHILD.

The "Manuscript Story" has been published in full, and comparisons between the same and the Book of Mormon may be made by anyone who has a mind to investigate the subject.[1]

[Footnote 1: For a fuller account of the Book of Mormon, see the author's "Articles of Faith," Lectures 14 and 15; published at Salt Lake City, Utah, 1913.]

CHAPTER II

But we have anticipated the current of events. With the publication of the Book of Mormon, opposition grew more intense toward the people who professed a belief in the testimony of Joseph Smith. On the 6th of April, 1830, the Church of Jesus Christ of Latter-day Saints was formally organized and thus took on a legal existence. The scene of this organization was Fayette, New York, and but six persons were directly concerned as participants. At that time there may have been and probably were many times that number who had professed adherence to the newly restored faith; but as the requirements of the law governing the formation of religious societies were satisfied by the application of six, only the specified number formally took part. Such was the beginning of the Church, soon to be so universally maligned. Its origin was small—a germ, an insignificant seed, hardly to be thought of as likely to arouse opposition. What was there to fear in the voluntary association of six men, avowedly devoted to peaceful pursuits and benevolent purposes? Yet a storm of persecution was threatened from the earliest day. At first but a family affair, opposition to the work has involved successively the town, the county, the state, the country, and today the "Mormon" question has been accorded extended consideration at the hands of the national government, and indeed most civilized nations have taken cognizance of the same.

Let us observe the contrast between the beginning and the present proportions of the Church. Instead of but six regularly affiliated members, and at most two score of adherents, the organization numbers today many hundred thousand souls. In place of a single hamlet, in the smallest corner of which the members could have congregated, there now are about seventy stakes of Zion and about seven hundred organized wards, each ward and stake with its full complement of officers and priesthood organizations. The practise of gathering its proselytes into one place prevents the building up and strengthening of foreign branches; and inasmuch as extensive and strong organizations are seldom met with abroad, very erroneous ideas exist concerning the strength of the Church. Nevertheless, the mustard seed, among the smallest of all seeds, has attained the proportions of a tree, and the birds of the air are nesting in its branches; the acorn is now an oak offering protection and the sweets of satisfaction to every earnest pilgrim journeying its way for truth.

From the organization of the Church, the spirit of emigration rested upon the people. Their eyes were from the first turned in anticipation toward the evening sun—not merely that the work of proselyting should be carried on in the west, but that the headquarters of the Church should be there established. The Book of Mormon had taught the people the true origin and destiny of the American Indians; and toward this dark-skinned remnant of a once mighty people, the missionaries of "Mormonism" early turned their eyes, and with their eyes went their hearts and their hopes.

Within three months from the beginning, the Church had missionaries among the Lamanites. It is notable that the Indian tribes have generally regarded the religion of the Latter-day Saints with favor, seeing in the Book of Mormon striking agreement with their own traditions.

The first well-established seat of the Church was in the pretty little town of Kirtland, Ohio, almost within sight of Lake Erie; and here soon rose the first temple of modern times. Among their many other peculiarities, the Latter-day Saints are characterized as a temple-building people, as history proves the Israel of ancient times to have been. In the days of their infancy as a Church, while in the thrall of poverty, and amidst the persecution and direful threats of lawless hordes, they laid the cornerstone, and in less than three years thereafter they celebrated the dedication of the Kirtland Temple, a structure at once beautiful and imposing. Even before this time, however, populous settlements of Latter-day Saints had been made in Jackson County, Missouri; and in the town of Independence a site for a great temple had been selected and purchased; but though the ground has been dedicated with solemn ceremony, the people have not as yet built thereon.

Within two years of its dedication, the temple in Kirtland was abandoned by the people, who were compelled to flee for their lives before the onslaughts of mobocrats; but a second temple, larger and more beautiful than the first, soon reared its spires in the city of Nauvoo, Illinois. This structure was destroyed by fire, but the temple-building spirit was not to be quenched, and in the vales of Utah today are four magnificent temple edifices. The last completed, which was the first begun, is situated in Salt Lake City, and is one of the wonders and beauties of that city by the great salt sea.[2]

[Footnote 2: For a detailed account of modern temples, with numerous pictorial views, see "The House of the Lord," by the present author; Salt Lake City, Utah, 1912.]

To the fervent Latter-day Saint, a temple is not simply a church building, a house for religious assembly. Indeed the "Mormon" temples are rarely used as places of general gatherings. They are in one sense educational institutions, regular courses of lectures and instruction being maintained in some of them; but they are specifically for baptisms and ordinations, for sanctifying prayer, and for the most sacred ceremonies and rites of the Church, particularly in the vicarious work for the dead which is a characteristic of "Mormon" faith. And who that has gazed upon these splendid shrines will say that the people who can do so much in poverty and tribulation are insincere? Bigoted they may seem to those who believe not as they do; fanatics they may be to multitudes who like the proud Pharisee of old thank God they are not as these; but insincere they cannot be, even in the judgment of their bitterest opponent, if he be a creature of reason.

The clouds of persecution thickened in Ohio as the intolerant zeal of mobs found frequent expression; numerous charges, trivial and serious, were made against the leaders of the Church, and they were repeatedly brought before the courts, only to be liberated on the usual finding of no cause for action. Meanwhile the march to the west was maintained. Soon thousands of converts had rented or purchased homes in Missouri—Independence, Jackson County, being their center; but from the first, they were unpopular among the Missourians. Their system of equal rights with their marked disapproval of every species of aristocratic separation and self-aggrandizement was declared to be a species of communism, dangerous to the state. An inoffensive journalistic organ, *The Star*, published for the purpose of properly presenting the religious tenets of the people, was made the particular object of the mob's rage; the house of its publisher was razed to the ground, the press and type were confiscated, and the editor and his family maltreated. An absurd story was circulated and took firm hold of the masses that the Book of Mormon promised the western lands to the people of the Church, and that they intended to take possession of these lands by force. Throughout the book of revelations regarded by the people as law specially directed to them, they are told to save their riches that they may purchase the inheritance promised them of God. Everywhere are they told to maintain peace; the sword is never offered as their symbol of conquest. Their gathering is to be like that of the Jews at Jerusalem—a pacific one, and in their taking possession of what they regard as a land of promise, no one previously located there shall be denied his rights.

A spirit of fierce persecution raged in Jackson and surrounding counties of Missouri. An appeal was made to the executive of the state, but little encouragement was returned. The lieutenant- governor, Lilburn W. Boggs, afterward governor, was a pronounced "Mormon"-hater, and throughout the period of the troubles, he manifested sympathy with the persecutors.

One of the circuit judges who was asked to issue a peace warrant refused to do so, but advised the "Mormons" to arm themselves and meet the force of the outlaws with organized resistance. This advice was not pleasing to the Latter-day Saints, whose religion enjoined tolerance and peace; but they so far heeded it as to arm a small force; and when the outlaws next came upon them, the people were not entirely unprepared. A "Mormon" rebellion was now proclaimed. The people had been goaded to desperation. The militia was ordered out, and the "Mormons" were disarmed. The mob was unrestrained in its eagerness for revenge. The "Mormons" engaged able lawyers to institute and maintain legal proceedings against their foes, and this step, the right to which one would think could be denied no American citizen, called forth such an uproar of popular wrath as to affect almost the entire state.

It was winter; but the inclemency of the year only suited the better the purpose of the oppressor. Homes were destroyed, men torn from their families were brutally beaten, tarred and feathered;

women with babes in their arms were forced to flee half-clad into the solitude of the prairie to escape from mobocratic violence. Their sufferings have never yet been fitly chronicled by human scribe. Making their way across the river, most of the refugees found shelter among the more hospitable people of Clay County, and afterward established themselves in Caldwell County, therein founding the city of Far West. County and state judges, the governor, and even the President of the United States, were appealed to in turn for redress. The national executive, Andrew Jackson, while expressing sympathy for the persecuted people, deplored his lack of power to interfere with the administration or non-administration of state laws; the national officials could do nothing; the state officials would do naught.

But the expulsion from Jackson County was but a prelude to the tragedy soon to follow. A single scene of the bloody drama is known as the Haun's Mill massacre. A small settlement had been founded by "Mormon" families on Shoal Creek, and here on the 30th of October, 1838, a company of two hundred and forty fell upon the hapless settlers and butchered a score. No respect was paid to age or sex; grey heads, and infant lips that scarcely had learned to lisp a word, vigorous manhood and immature youth, mother and maiden, fared alike in the scene of carnage, and their bodies were thrown into an old well.

In October, 1838, the Governor of Missouri, the same Lilburn W. Boggs, issued his infamous exterminating order, and called upon the militia of the state to execute it. The language of this document, signed by the executive of a sovereign state of the Union, declared that the "Mormons" must be driven from the state or exterminated. Be it said to the honor of some of the officers entrusted with the terrible commission, that when they learned its true significance they resigned their authority rather than have anything to do with what they designated a cold-blooded butchery. But tools were not wanting, as indeed they never have been, for murder and its kindred outrages. What the heart of man can conceive, the hand of man will find a way to execute. The awful work was carried out with dread dispatch. Oh, what a record to read; what a picture to gaze upon; how awful the fact! An official edict offering expatriation or death to a peaceable community with no crime proved against them, and guilty of no offense other than that of choosing to differ in opinion from the masses! American school boys read with emotions of horror of the Albigenses, driven, beaten and killed, with a papal legate directing the butchery; and of the Vaudois, hunted and hounded like beasts as the effect of a royal decree; and they yet shall read in the history of their own country of scenes as terrible as these in the exhibition of injustice and inhuman hate.

In the dread alternative offered them, the people determined again to abandon their homes; but whither should they go? Already they had fled before the lawless oppressor over well nigh half a continent; already were they on the frontiers of the country that they had regarded as the land of promised liberty. Thus far every move had carried them westward, but farther west they could not go unless they went entirely beyond the country of their birth, and gave up their hope of protection under the Constitution, which to them had ever been an inspired instrument, the majesty of which, as they had never doubted, would be some day vindicated, even to securing for them the rights of American citizens. This time their faces were turned toward the east; and a host numbering from ten to twelve thousand, including many women and children, abandoned their homes and fled before their murderous pursuers, reddening the snow with bloody footprints as they journeyed. They crossed the Mississippi and sought protection on the soil of Illinois. There their sad condition evoked for a time general commiseration.

The press of the state denounced the treatment of the people by the Missourians and vindicated the character of the "Mormons" as peaceable and law-abiding citizens. College professors published expressions of their horror over the cruel crusade; state officials, including even the governor, gave substantial evidence of their sympathy and good feeling. This lull in the storm of outrage that had so long raged about them offered a strange contrast to their usual treatment. Let it not be thought that all the people of Illinois were their friends; from the first, opposition was manifest, but their condition was so greatly bettered that they might have thought the advent of their Zion to be near at hand.

I stated that professional men, and even college professors raised their voices in commiseration of the "Mormon" situation and in denouncing the "Mormon" oppressors. Prof. Turner of Illinois College wrote:

> Who began the quarrel? Was it the "Mormons?" Is it not notorious on the contrary that they were hunted like wild beasts from county to county before they made any resistance? Did they ever, as a body, refuse obedience to the laws, when called upon to do so, until driven to desperation by repeated threats and assaults by the mob? Did the state ever make one decent effort to defend them as fellow-citizens in their rights or to redress their wrongs? Let the conduct of its governors and attorneys and the fate of their final petitions answer! Have any who plundered and openly insulted the "Mormons" ever been brought to the punishment due to their crimes? Let boasting murderers of begging and helpless infancy answer! Has the state ever remunerated even those known to be innocent for the loss of either their property or their arms? Did either the pulpit or the press through the state raise a note of remonstrance or alarm? Let the clergymen who abetted and the editors who encouraged the mob answer!

As a sample of the press comments against the brutality of the Missourians I quote a paragraph from the Quincy *Argus*, March 16, 1839:

> We have no language sufficiently strong for the expression of our indignation and shame at the recent transaction in a sister state, and that state, Missouri, a state of which we had long been proud, alike for her men and history, but now so fallen that we could wish her star stricken from the bright constellation of the Union. We say we know of no language sufficiently strong for the expression of our shame and abhorrence of her recent conduct. She has written her own character in letters of blood, and stained it by acts of merciless cruelty and brutality that the waters of ages cannot efface. It will be observed that an organized

mob, aided by many of the civil and military officers of Missouri, with Gov. Boggs at their head, have been the prominent actors in this business, incited too, it appears, against the "Mormons" by political hatred, and by the additional motives of plunder and revenge. They have but too well put in execution their threats of extermination and expulsion, and fully wreaked their vengeance on a body of industrious and enterprising men, who had never wronged nor wished to wrong them, but on the contrary had ever comported themselves as good and honest citizens, living under the same laws, and having the same right with themselves to the sacred immunities of life, liberty and property.

CHAPTER III

Settling in and about the obscure village of Commerce, the "Mormon" refugees soon demonstrated anew the marvelous recuperative power with which they were endowed, and a city seemed to spring from the earth. Nauvoo—the City Beautiful—was the name given to this new abiding place. It was situated but a few miles from Quincy, in a bend of the majestic river, giving the town three water fronts. It seemed to nestle there as if the Father of Waters was encircling it with his mighty arm. Soon a glorious temple crowned the hill up which the city had run in its rapid growth. Their settlements extended into Iowa, then a territory. The governors of both Iowa and Ohio testified to the worthiness of the Latter-day Saints as citizens, and pledged them the protection of the commonwealth. The city of Nauvoo was chartered by the state of Illinois, and the rights of local self-government were assured to its citizens.

A military organization, the "Nauvoo Legion," was authorized, and the establishment of a university was provided for; both these organizations were successfully effected. It was here that a memorial was prepared and sent to the national government, reciting the outrages of Missouri, and asking reparation. Joseph Smith himself, the head of the delegation, had a personal interview with President Van Buren, in which the grievances of the Latter-day Saints were presented. Van Buren replied in words that will not be forgotten, "Your cause is just, but I can do nothing for you."

The peaceful conditions at first characteristic of their Illinois settlement were not to continue. The element of political influence asserted itself and the "Mormons" bade fair to soon hold the balance of power in local affairs. The characteristic unity, so marked in connection with every phase of the people's existence, promised too much; immigration into Hancock county was continuous, and the growing power of the Latter-day Saints was viewed with apprehension. With this as the true motive, many pretexts for annoyance were found; and arrests, trials, and acquittals were common experiences of the Church officers.

A charge, which promised to prove as devoid of foundation as had the excuses for the fifty arrests preceding it, led Joseph Smith, president of the Church, and Hyrum Smith, the patriarch, to again surrender themselves to the officers of the law. They were taken to Carthage, Joseph having declared to friends his belief that he was going to the slaughter. Governor Ford gave to the prisoners his personal guarantee for their safety; but mob violence was supreme, more mighty than the power of the state militia placed there to guard the prison; and these men were shot to death, even while under the governor's plighted pledge of protection. Hyrum fell first; and Joseph, appearing at one of the windows in the second story, received the leaden missiles of the besieging mob, which was led by a recreant though professed minister of the gospel. But the brutish passion of the mob was not yet sated; propping the body against a well-curb in the jail-yard, the murderers poured a volley of bullets into the corpse, and fled. Thus was the unholy vow of the mob fulfilled, that as law could not touch the "Mormon" leaders, powder and ball should. John Taylor, who became years afterward president of the Church, was in the jail at the same time; he received four bullets, and was left supposedly dead.

Joseph Smith had been more than the ecclesiastical leader; his presence and personality had been ever powerful as a stimulus to the hearts of the people; none knew his personal power better than the members of his own flock, unless indeed it were the wolves who were ever seeking to harry the fold. It had been the boast of anti-"Mormons" that with Joseph Smith removed, the Church would crumble to pieces of itself. In the personality of their leader, it was thought, lay the secret of the people's strength; and like the Philistines, the enemy struck at the supposed bond of power. Terrible as was the blow of the fearful fatality, the Church soon emerged from its despairing state of poignant grief, and rose mightier than before. It is the faith of this people that while the work of God on earth is carried on by men, yet mortals are but instruments in the Creator's hands for the accomplishment of divine purposes. The death of the president disorganized the First Presidency of the Church; but the official body next in authority, the Council of the Twelve, stepped to the front, and the progress of the Church was unhindered. The work of the ministry was not arrested; the people paused but long enough to bury their dead and clear their eyes from the blinding tears that fell.

Let us take a retrospective glance at this unusual man. Though his opponents deny him the divine commission with which his friends believe he was charged, they all, friends and foes alike, admit that he was a great man. Through the testimony of his life's work and the sanctifying seal of his martyrdom, thousands have come to acknowledge him all that he professed to be—a messenger from God to the people. He is not without admirers among men who deny the truth of his principles and the faith of his people.

A historical writer of the time, Josiah Quincy, a few weeks after the martyrdom, wrote:

> It is by no means improbable that some future text book for the use of generations yet unborn, will contain a question something like this: "What historical American of the nineteenth century has exerted the most powerful influence upon the destinies of his countrymen?" And it is by no means impossible that the answer to that interrogatory may be thus written—"Joseph Smith, the Mormon Prophet." And the reply, absurd as it doubtless seems to most men now living, may be an obvious commonplace to their descendants. History deals in surprises and paradoxes quite as startling as this. A man who established a religion in this age of free debate, who was and is today accepted by hundreds of thousands as a direct emissary from the Most High—such a rare human being is not to be disposed of by pelting his memory with unsavory epithets. * * * The most vital questions Americans are asking each other today, have to deal with this man and what he has left us. * * * Joseph Smith, claiming to be an inspired teacher, faced adversity such as few men have been called to meet, enjoyed a brief season of prosperity such as few men have ever attained, and finally * * * went cheerfully to a martyr's death. When he surrendered his person to Governor Ford, in order to prevent the shedding of blood, the

> Prophet had a presentiment of what was before him. "I am going like a lamb to the slaughter," he is reported to have said, "but I am as calm as a summer's morning. I have a conscience void of offense, and shall die innocent."

The "Mormon" people regarded it as a duty to make every proper effort to bring the perpetrators of the foul assassination of their leaders to justice; sixty names were presented to the local grand jury, and of the persons so designated, nine were indicted. After a farcical semblance of a trial, these were acquitted, and thus was notice, sanctioned by the constituted authority of the law, served upon all anti-"Mormons" of Illinois, that they were safe in any assault they might choose to make on the subjects of their hate. The mob was composed of apt pupils in the learning of this lesson. Personal outrages were of every-day occurrence; husbandmen were captured in their fields, beaten, tortured, until they barely had strength left to promise compliance with the demands of their assailants,—that they would leave the state. Houses were fired while the tenants were wrapped in uneasy slumber within; indeed, one entire town, that of Morley, was by such incendiarism reduced to ashes. Women and children were aroused in the night, and compelled to flee unclad or perish in their burning dwellings.

But what of the internal work of the Church during these trying periods? As the winds of winter, the storms of the year's deepest night, do but harden and strengthen the mountain pine, whose roots strike the deeper, whose branches thicken, whose twigs multiply by the inclemency that would be fatal to the exotic palm, raised by man with hot-house nursing, so the new sect continued its growth, partly in spite of, partly because of, the storms to which it was subjected. It was no green-house growth, struggling for existence in a foreign clime, but a fit plant for the soil of a free land; and there existed in the minds of unprejudiced observers not a doubt as to its vitality. The Church soon found its equilibrium again after the shock of its cruel experience. Brigham Young, who for a decade had been identified with the cause, who had received his full share of persecution at mobocratic hands, now stood at the head of the presiding body in the priesthood of the Church. The effect of this man's wonderful personality, his surprising natural ability, and to the people, the proofs of his divine acceptance, were apparent from the first.

Migration from other states and from foreign shores continued to swell the "Mormon" band, and this but angered the oppressors the more. The members of the Church, recognizing the inevitable long before predicted by their murdered prophet, that the march of the Church would be westward, redoubled their efforts to complete the grand temple upon which they had not ceased to work through all the storms of persecution. This structure, solemnly dedicated to their God, they entered, and there received their anointings and their blessings; then they abandoned it to the desecration and self-condemning outrages of their foes. For the mob's decree had gone forth, that the "Mormons" must leave Illinois. After a few sanguinary encounters, the leaders of the people acceded to the demands of their assailants, and agreed to leave early in the following spring; but the departure was not speedy enough to suit, and the lawless persecution was waged the more ruthlessly.

Soon the soil of Illinois was free from "Mormon" tread; Nauvoo was deserted, her 20,000 inhabitants expatriated. Colonel Thomas L. Kane, a conspicuous figure at this stage of our country's history, was traveling eastward at the time, and reached Nauvoo shortly after its evacuation. In a lecture before the Historical Society of Pennsylvania, he related his experience in this sometime abode of the Saints. I paraphrase a portion of his eloquent address.

Sighting the city from the western shore of the mighty Mississippi, as it nestled in the river's encircling embrace, he crossed to its principal wharf, and, there to his surprise, found no soul to meet him. The stillness that everywhere prevailed was painful, broken only by an occasional faint echo of boisterous shout or ribald song from a distance. The town was in a dream, and the warrior trod lightly lest he wake it in affright, for he plainly saw that it had not slumbered long. No grass grew in the pavement joints; recent footprints were still distinct in the dusty thoroughfares. The visitor made his way unmolested into work-shops and smithies; tools lay as last used; on the carpenter's bench was the unfinished frame, on the floor were the shavings fresh and odorous; the wood was piled in readiness before the baker's oven; the blacksmith's forge was cold, but the shop looked as though the occupant had just gone off for a holiday. The gallant soldier entered gardens unchallenged by owner, human guard, or watchful dog; he might have supposed the people hidden or dead in their houses; but the doors were not fastened, and he entered to explore, there were fresh ashes on the hearth; no great accumulation of the dust of time was on floors or furniture; the awful quiet compelled him to tread a-tip-toe as if threading the aisles of an unoccupied cathedral. He hastened to the graveyard, though surely the city had not been depopulated by pestilence. No; there were a few stones newly set, some sods freshly turned in this sacred acre of God, but where can you find a cemetery of a living town with no such evidence of recent interment? There were fields of heavy grain, the bounteous harvest rotting on the ground; there were orchards dropping their rich and rosy fruit to spoil beneath; not a hand to gather or save.

But in a suburban corner, he came across the smoldering embers of a barbecue fire, with fragments of flesh and other remnants of a feast. Hereabout houses had been demolished; and there beyond, around the great temple that had first attracted his attention from the Iowa shore, armed men were bivouacked. This worthy representative of our country's service was challenged by the drunken crowd, and made to give an account of himself, and to answer for having crossed the river without a permit from the head of the band. Finding that he was a stranger, they related to him in fiendish glee their recent exploits of pillage, rapine, and murder. They conducted him through the temple; everywhere were marks of their brutish acts; its altars of prayer were broken; the baptismal font had been so "diligently desecrated as to render the apartment in which it was contained too noisome to abide in." There in the steeple close by the "scar of divine wrath" left by a recent thunderbolt, were broken covers of liquor and drinking vessels.

Sickened with the sight, disgusted with this spectacle of outrage, the colonel recrossed the river at nightfall, beating upward, for the wind had freshened. Attracted by a faint light near the bank, he approached the spot, there to find a few haggard faces surrounding one who seemed to be in the last stages of fever. The sufferer was partially protected by something like a tent made from a couple of bed sheets; and amid such environment, the spirit was pluming itself for flight. Making his way through this camp of misery, he heard the sobbings of children hungry and sick; there were men and women dying from wounds or disease, without a semblance of shelter or other physical comfort; wives in the pangs of maternity, ushering into the world innocent babes doomed to be motherless from their birth. And at intervals, to the ears of those outcasts, the sick and the dying, the wind brought the soul-piercing sounds of the reveling mob in the distant city, the scrap of vulgar song, the shocking oath, shrieked from the temple tower in the madness of drunken orgies.

This, however, was but the rear remnant of the' expatriated Christian band. The van was already far on its way toward the inviting wilderness of the all but unknown west. But the wanderers were not wholly without friends; certain Indian tribes, the Omahas and the Potawatomis, welcomed them to their lands, inviting them to camp within their territory during the coming winter. "Welcome," said these children of the forest, "we too have been driven from our pleasant homes east of the great river, to these damp and unhealthful bottoms; you now, white men, have been driven forth to the prairies; we are fellow-sufferers. Welcome, brothers."

In return much assistance was rendered by the white refugees to their, shall I say savage friends? If it was civilization the wanderers had left, then indeed might the red men of the forest have felt proud of their distinction. But the Indian agent, a Christian gentleman, ordered the "Mormons" to move on and leave the reservation which a kind government had provided for its red children. An order from President Polk, who had been appealed to by Colonel Kane, gave the people permission to remain for a short season. The government of Iowa had courteously assured them protection while passing through that territory. As soon as the people were well under way, a thorough organization was effected. Remembering the toilsome desert march from Egypt to Canaan, the people assumed the name, "Camp of Israel." The camp consisted of two main divisions, and each was sub-divided into companies of hundreds, fifties, and tens, with captains to direct. An officer with one hundred volunteers went ahead of the main body to select a route and prepare a road. At this time, there were over one thousand wagons of the "Mormons" rolling westward, and the line of march soon reached from the Mississippi to Council Bluffs. There were in the company not half enough draft animals for the arduous march, and but an insufficient number of able-bodied men to tend the camps. The women had to assist in driving teams and stock, and in other labors of the journey. Yet with their characteristic cheerfulness the people made the best, and that proved to be a great deal, out of their lot. When the camp halted, a city seemed to spring as if by magic from the prairie soil. Concerts and social gatherings were usual features of the evening rests.

But another great event disturbed the equanimity of the camp. War had broken out between Mexico and the United States. General Taylor's victories in the early stages of the strife had been all but decisive, but the Republic was on march to the western ocean and the provinces of New Mexico and California were in her path. These two provinces comprised in addition to the territory now designated by those names, Utah, Nevada, portions of Wyoming and Colorado, as also Arizona; while Oregon, then claimed by Great Britain, included Washington, Idaho, and portions of Montana and Wyoming. It was the plan of the national administration to occupy these provinces at the earliest moment possible; and a call was made upon the "Mormon" refugees to contribute to the general force by furnishing a battalion of five hundred men to take part in the war with Mexico. The surprise which the message of the government officer produced in the camp amounted almost to dismay. Five hundred men fit to bear arms to be drafted from that camp! What would become of the rest? Already women and boys had been pressed into service to do the work of men; already the sick and the halt had been neglected; and many graves marked the path they had traversed, whose tenants had passed to their last sleep through lack of care.

But how long did they hesitate? Scarcely an hour; it was the call of their country. True, they were even then leaving the national soil, but not of their own will. To them their country was and is the promised land, the Lord's chosen place, the land of Zion. "You shall have your battalion," said Brigham Young to Captain Allen, the muster officer, "and if there are not young men enough, we will take the old men, and if they are not enough, we will take the women." Within a week from the time President Polk's message was received, the entire force, in all five hundred and forty-nine souls, was on the march to Fort Leavenworth. Their path from the Missouri to the Pacific led them over two thousand miles, much of this distance being measured through deserts, which prior to that time had not been trodden by civilized foot.

Colonel Cooke, the commander of the "Mormon" Battalion, declared, "History may be searched in vain for an equal march of infantry." Many were disabled through the severity of the march, and numerous cases of sickness and death were chronicled. General Kearney and his successor, Governor R. B. Mason, as military commandants of California, spoke in high praise of this organization, and in their official reports declared that they had made efforts to prolong the battalion's term of service; but most of the men chose to rejoin their families as soon as they could secure their honorable discharge.

But to return to the Camp of Israel: A pioneer party, consisting of a hundred and forty and four, preceded the main body; and the line of the migrating hosts soon stretched from the Missouri to the valley of the Great Salt Lake. Wagons there were, as also some horses and men, but all too few for the journey; and a great part of the company walked the full thousand miles across the great plains and the forbidding deserts of the west. In the Black Hills region, the pioneers were delayed a week at the Platte, a stream, which, though usually fordable at this point was now so swollen as to make fording impossible. Here, too, their provisions were well nigh exhausted. Game had not been plentiful, and the "Mormon" pioneers were threatened with the direst privations. In their slow march they had been passed by a number of well-equipped parties, some of them from Missouri bound for the Pacific; but most of these were overtaken on the easterly side of the river. Amongst the effects of the "Mormon" party was a leathern boat, which on water served the legitimate purpose of its maker and on land was made to do service as a wagon box. This, together with rafts specially constructed, was now put to good use in ferrying across the river not alone themselves and their little property, but the other companies and their loads. For this service they were well paid in camp provisions.

Thus, the expatriated pioneers found themselves relieved from want with their meal sacks replenished in the heart of the wilderness. Many may call it superstition, but some will regard it as did the thankful travelers—an interposition of Providence, and an answer to their prayers—an event to be compared, they said, to the feeding of Israel with manna in the wilderness of old.

After over three months' journeying, the pioneer company reached the valley of the Great Salt Lake; and at the first sight of it, Brigham Young declared it to be the halting place—the gathering center for the Saints. But what was there inviting in this wilderness spread out like a scroll barren of inviting message, and empty but for the picture it presented of wondrous scenic grandeur? Looking from the Wasatch barrier, the colonists gazed upon a scene of entrancing though forbidding beauty. A barren, arid plain, rimmed by mountains like a literal basin, still occupied in its lowest parts by the dregs of what had once filled it to the brim; no green meadows, not a tree worthy the name, scarce a patch of greensward to entice the adventurous wanderers into the valley. The slopes were covered with sagebrush, relieved by patches of chaparral oak and squawbush; the wild sunflower lent its golden hue to intensify the sharp contrasts. Off to the westward lay the lake, making an impressive, uninviting picture in its severe, unliving beauty; from its blue wastes somber peaks rose as precipitous islands, and about the shores of this dead sea were saline flats that told of the scorching heat and thirsty atmosphere of this parched region. A turbid river ran from south to north athwart the valley, "dividing it in twain," as a historian of the day has written, "as if the vast bowl in the intense heat of the Master Potter's fires, in process of formation had cracked asunder." Small streams of water started in rippling haste from the snow-caps of the mountains toward the lake, but most of them were devoured by the thirsty sands of the valley before their journey was half completed.

Such was the scene of desolation that greeted the pioneer band. A more forsaken spot they had not passed in all their wanderings. And is this the promised land? This is the very place of which Bridger spake when he proffered a thousand dollars in gold for the first bushel of grain that could be raised here. With such a Canaan spread out before them, was it not wholly pardonable if some did sigh with longing for the leeks and flesh-pots of the Egypt they had left, or wished to pass by this land and seek a fairer home? Two of the three women who belonged to the party were utterly disappointed. "Weak, worn, and weary as I am," said one of these heroines, "I would rather push on another thousand miles than stay here."

But the voice of their leader was heard. "The very place," said Brigham Young, and in his prophetic mind there rose a vision of what was to come. Not for a moment did he doubt the future. He saw a multitude of towns and cities, hamlets and villas filling this and neighboring valleys, with the fairest of all, a city whose beauty of situation, whose wealth of resource should become known throughout the world, rising from the most arid site of the burning desert before him, hard by the barren salt shores of the watery waste. There in the very heart of the parched wilderness should stand the House of the Lord, with other temples in valleys beyond the horizon of his gaze.

Within a few hours after the arrival of the vanguard upon the banks of what is now known as City Creek—the mountain stream which today furnishes Salt Lake City part of her water supply—plows were put to work; but the hard-baked soil, never before disturbed by the efforts of man to till, refused to yield to the share. A dam was thrown across the stream and the softening liquid was spread upon the flat that had been chosen for the first fields. The planting season had already well nigh passed, and not a day could be lost. Potatoes and other seed were put in, and the land was again flooded. Such was the beginning of the irrigation system, which soon became co-extensive with the area occupied by the "Mormon" settlers, a system which under the blessing of Providence, has proved to be the veritable magic touch by which the desert has been made a field of richness and a garden of beauty; a system which now after many decades of successful trial is held up by the nation's wise and great ones to be the one practicable method of reclaiming our country's vast domains of arid lands. It was on the 24th of July, 1847, that the main part of the pioneer band entered the valley of the Great Salt Lake, and that day of the year is observed as a legal holiday in Utah. From that time to the present, the stream of immigration to these valleys has never ceased.

CHAPTER IV

The dangers of the first company's migration were surpassed by those of parties who subsequently braved the terrors of the plains. In their enthusiasm to reach the gathering place of their people, many of the Latter-day Saints set out from Iowa, where railway facilities had their termination, with hand-carts only as a means of conveyance. Today there are living in the smiling vales of Utah, men and women who then as boys and girls trudged wearily across the prairies, dragging the lumbering carts that contained their entire provision against starvation and freezing. Such handcart companies were organized with care; a limited amount of freight was allowed to each division; milch cattle and a very few draft-animals, with wagons for conveying the heavier baggage and to carry the sick, were assigned. The tale of those dreary marches has never yet been told; the song of the heroism and sacrifice displayed by these pilgrims for conscience sake is awaiting a singer worthy the theme. Wading the streams with carts in tow, or in cases of unfordable streams, stopping to construct rafts; at times living on reduced rations of but a few ounces of meal per day; lying down at night with a prayer in the heart that they wake no more on earth, a prayer which had its fulfilment in hundreds of cases; the dying heaving their parting sighs in the arms of loved ones who were soon to follow, they journeyed on.

The inevitable catastrophes and accidents of travel robbed them of their substance. Hostile savages stampeded their cattle, or openly attacked and plundered the trains. But on they went, never swerving from the course. These later companies needed no chart nor compass to guide them over the desert; the road was plain from the marks of former camps, and yet more so from the graves of friends and loved ones who had started before on the road to the earthly Zion and found that it led them to the martyr's entrance to heaven, graves that were marked perhaps but by a rude inscription cut on a pole or a board. And even these narrow lodgings had not been left inviolate; the wolves of the plains had too often succeeded in unearthing and rending the bodies. Every company thus made the course the plainer; each of them added to the silent population of the desert; sometimes half a score were interred at one camp, and of one company over a fourth were thus left beside the prairie road. Now we traverse the self-same track in a day and a night, reclining on luxurious cushions of ease, covering fifty miles while dining in luxury; and we avert the ennui of the journey by berating the railway company for lack of speed.

Relief trains were continually on the way between the valley of the Salt Lake and the Missouri; and the remnants of many a company were saved from what appeared to be certain destruction by the opportune arrival of these rescuing parties. Such relief came from those who were themselves destitute and almost starving. Brigham Young with a few of the chief officials of the Church, and aids, returned eastward on such an errand of rescue within a few weeks after first reaching the valley. The region to which the early settlers came was in no wise a typical land of promise; it did not flow spontaneously with milk and honey.

Drought and unseasonable frosts made the first year's farming experiments but doubtful successes, and in the succeeding spring the land was visited by the devastating plague of the Rocky Mountain crickets. They swarmed down in innumerable hordes upon the fields, destroying the growing crops as they advanced, devouring all before them, leaving the land a desert in their track. The people scarcely knew how to withstand the assault of this new foe; they drove the marauders into trenches there to be drowned or burned; men, women and every child that could swing a stick, were called to the ranks in this insect war; and with all their fighting, the people forgot not to pray for deliverance, and they fasted, too, for the best of reasons.

And as they watched, and prayed, and worked, they saw approaching from the north and west a veritable host of winged creatures of more formidable proportions still; and these bore down upon the fields as though coming to complete the devastation. But see! these are of the color that betokens peace; they are the gulls, white and beautiful, advancing upon the hosts of the black destroyers. Falling upon the people's foes, they devoured them by the thousand, and when filled to repletion, disgorged and feasted again.

And they did not stop till the crickets were destroyed. Again the skeptic will say this was but chance; but the people accepted that chance as a providential ruling in their behalf, and reverently did they give thanks.

Today the wanton killing of a gull in Utah is an offense in law; but stronger than legal proscription, more powerful than fear of judicial penalties, is the popular sentiment in favor of these white-winged deliverers. Every year come these graceful creatures to spend the springtime in the fields and upon the lakes of Utah; and right well do they feel their welcome, for they are habitually so tame and fearless that they may almost be touched by the hand before they take flight.

By the autumn of 1848, five thousand people had already reached the valley, and the food problem was a most difficult one. The winter was severe; and famine, stark and inexorable, threw its dread shadow over the people. There seemed to be an entry in the book of fate that every possible test of human endurance and integrity should be applied to this pilgrim band. Without distinction as to former station, they went out and dug the roots of weeds, gathered the tenderest of the coarse grass, thistles, and wild berries, and thus did they subsist; upon such did they feast with thanksgiving, until a less scanty harvest relieved their wants.

It was at this time that the gold fever was at its height, a consequence of the discovery of the precious metal in California, in which discovery, indeed, certain members of the disbanded "Mormon" Battalion, working their way eastward, were most prominent. Some of the "Mormon" settlers, becoming infected with the malady, hastened westward, but the counsel of the Church authorities prevailed to keep all but a few at home. These people had not left the country of their birth or adoption to seek gold; nor bright jewels of the mine; nor the wealth of seas; nor the spoils of war; they sought and believed they had found, a faith's pure shrine. But the gold-seekers hastening westward, and the successful miners returning eastward, halted at the "Mormon" settlements and there replenished their supplies, leaving their gold to enrich the people of the desert.

But of what use is gold in the wilderness! In the old legend a famishing Arab, finding a well filled bag upon the sand was thrilled with joy at the thought of dates—his bread; and then was cast into the depths of despair when he realized that he had found nothing but a bag of costly pearls. The settlers by the lake needed horses and wagons, tools, implements of husbandry and building; and gold was valuable only as it represented a means of obtaining these. Gold became so plentiful and was withal so worthless in the desert colony that men refused to take it for their labor. The yellow metal was collected in buckets and exported to the States in exchange for the goods so much desired. Merchandise brought in by caravans of "prairie schooners," was sold as fast as it could be put out; and strict rules were enforced allowing but a proportionate amount to each purchaser.

Within a few months after the first settlement of Utah, public schools were established; and one of the early acts of the provisional government was to grant a charter to the Deseret University, now known as the University of Utah.

Up to 1849, Utah had no political history. Settling in a Mexican province, the contest to determine its future ownership by the United States then in progress, the people in common with most pioneer communities established their own form of government. But in February, 1848, the treaty of Guadeloupe Hidalgo gave California to the United States; months passed, however, before the news of the change reached the west. Early in 1849, a call had been issued to "all the citizens of that portion of Upper California lying to the east of the Sierra Nevada mountains" to meet in convention at Great Salt Lake City; and there a petition was prepared asking of Congress the rights of self-government; and pending action, a temporary regime was established, under the name of the Provisional Government of the State of Deseret.

"Utah" was not the choice of the people as the name of their state; that word served but to recall the degraded tribes who had contested the settlement of the valleys. Deseret, a Book of Mormon name for the honey bee, was more appropriate. The petition of the people was denied in part, and, in 1850 was established the territorial form of government in Utah. Concerning the period of the provisional government, such men as Gunnison, Stansbury, and other federal officials on duty in the west, have recorded their praises of the

"Mormon" colonists in official reports. But with the un-American system of territorial government came troubles.

At first, many of the territorial officials were appointed from among the settlers themselves; thus, Brigham Young was the first governor; but strangers, who knew not the people nor their ways, filled with prejudice from the false reports they had heard, came from the east to govern the colonists in the desert. Of the federal appointees thus forced upon the people of Utah, many made for themselves most unenviable records.

Some of them were broken politicians, professional office-seekers, with no desire but to secure the greatest possible gain out of their appointment. With effrontery that would shock the modesty of a savage, the non-"Mormon" party adopted and flagrantly displayed the carpet-bag as the badge of their profession. But not all the officials sent to Utah from afar were of this type; some of them were honorable and upright men, and amongst this class the "Mormon" people reckon a number who, while opposed to their religious tenets, were nevertheless sincere and honest in the opposition they evinced.

In the early part of 1857, the published libels upon the people received many serious additions, the principal of which was promulgated in connection with the resignation of Judge Drummond of the Utah federal court. In his last letter to the United States attorney-general, he declared that his life was no longer safe in Utah, and that he had been compelled to flee from his bench; but the most serious charge of all was that the people had destroyed the records of the court, and that they had resented, with hostile demonstration, his protests; in short, that justice was dethroned in Utah, and that the people were in a state of open rebellion.

With mails three months apart, news traveled slowly; but as soon as word of this infamous charge reached Salt Lake City, the clerk of the court, Judge Drummond's clerk, sent a letter by express to the attorney-general, denying under oath the judge's statements, and attesting the declaration with official seal. The records, he declared, had been untouched except by official hands, and from the time of the court's establishment the files had been safe and were then in his personal keeping. But, before the clerk's communication had reached its destination, so difficult is it for stately truth to overtake flitting falsehood, the mischief had been done. Upon the most prejudiced reports utterly unfounded in fact, with a carelessness which even his personal and political friends found no ample means of explaining away, President Buchanan allowed himself to be persuaded that a "Mormon" rebellion existed, and ordered an army of over two thousand men to proceed straightway to Utah to subdue the rebels. Successors to the governor and other territorial officials were appointed, among whom there was not a single resident of Utah; and the military force was charged with the duty of installing the foreign appointees.

With great dispatch and under cover of secrecy, so that the Utah rebels might be taken by surprise, the army set out on the march. Before the troops reached the Rocky Mountains, the sworn statement from the clerk of the supreme court of Utah denying the charges made by Judge Drummond became public property; and about the same time men who had come from Utah to New York direct, published over their own signatures a declaration that all was peaceful in and about the settlements of Utah. The public eye began to twitch, and soon to open wide; the conviction was growing that someone had blundered. But to retract would be a plain confession of error; blunders must be covered up.

Let us leave the soldiers on their westward march, and ascertain how the news of the projected invasion reached the people of Utah, and what effect the tidings produced. Certain "Mormon" business agents, operating in Missouri, heard of the hostile movement. At first they were incredulous, but when the overland mail carrier from the west delivered his pouch and obtained his receipt, but was refused the bag of Utah mail with the postmaster's statement that he had been ordered to hold all mail for Utah, there seemed no room for doubt. Two of the Utahns immediately hastened westward.

On the 24th of July, 1857, the people had assembled in celebration of Pioneer Day. Silver Lake, a mountain gem set amidst the snows and forests and towering peaks of the Cottonwoods, had been selected as a fitting site for the festivities. The Stars and Stripes streamed above the camp; bands played; choirs sang; there were speeches, and picnics, and prayers. Experiences were compared as to the journeyings on the plains; stories were told of the shifts to which the people had been put by the vicissitudes of famine; but these dread experiences seemed to them now like a dream of the night; on this day all were happy. Were they not safe from savage foes both red and white? There had been peace for a season; and their desert homes were already smiling in wealth of flower and tree; the wilderness was blossoming under their feet; their consciences were void of offense toward their fellows. Yet at that very hour, all unbeknown to themselves, and without the opportunity of speaking a word in defense, these people had been convicted of insurrection and treason.

It was midday and the festivities were at their height, when a party of men rode into camp and sought an interview with Governor Young. Three of them had plainly ridden hard and far; they gave their report;—an armed force of thousands was at that hour approaching the territory; the boasts of officers and men as to what they would do when they found themselves in "Mormon" towns were reported; and these stories called up, in the minds of those who heard, the dread scenes of Far West and Nauvoo. Had these colonists of the wilderness not gone far enough to satisfy the hatred of their fellow-citizens in this republic of liberty? They had halted between the civilization of the east and that of the west, they had fled from the country that refused them a home, and now the nation would eject them from their desert lodgings.

A council was called and the situation was freely discussed. Had they not seen, lo, these many times, organized battalions and companies surpassing fiendish mobs in villainy? The evidence warranted their conclusion that invasion meant massacre. With tense calmness the plan of action was decided upon. It was the general conviction that war was inevitable, and it was decided to resist to the last. Then, if the army forced its way into the valleys of Utah on hostile purpose bent, it should find the land as truly a desert as it was when the pioneers first took possession. To this effect was the decision:—We have built cities in the east for our foes to occupy; our very temples have been desecrated and destroyed by them; but, with the help of Israel's God, we will prevent them enriching themselves with the spoils of our labors in these mountain retreats.

There seemed to be no room for doubt that war was about to break upon them; and with such a prospect, men may be expected to take every advantage of their situation. Brigham Young was still governor of Utah, and the militia was subject to his order. Promptly he proclaimed the territory under martial law, and forbade any armed body to cross its boundaries. Echo Canyon, the one promising route of ingress, was fortified. In those defiles an army might easily be stopped by a few; ammunition stations were established; provisions were cached; boulders were collected upon the cliffs beneath which the invaders must pass if they held to their purpose of forcing an entrance. The people had been roused to desperation, and force was to be met with force. In the settlements, combustibles were placed in readiness, and if the worst came, every "Mormon" house would be reduced to ashes, every tree would be hewn down.

With an experience of suffering that would have well served a better cause, this picked detachment of the United States army made its way to the Green River country; and there, counting well the cost of proceeding farther, went into camp at Fort Bridger. Many of the troops had almost perished in the storms, for it was late in November, and the winter had closed in early. Colonel Cooke reported to the commandant that half his horses had perished through cold and lack of food; hundreds of beef cattle had died; yet the region was so wild and forbidding that scarcely a wolf ventured there to glut itself upon the carcasses. In Cooke's own words we read that for thirty miles the road was blocked with carcasses—and "with abandoned and shattered property, they mark, perhaps beyond example in history, the steps of an advancing army with the horrors of a disastrous retreat."

With the army traveled the new federal appointees to offices in the territory. Cumming, the governor-to-be, issued a proclamation from his dug-out lodgings, and sent it to Salt Lake City by courier; he signed it as "Governor of Utah Territory." This but belittled him, for by the very terms of the Organic Act, to uphold which was the professed purpose of his coming, he was not governor until the oath of office had been duly administered and subscribed. A few days later he went before his fellow-sufferer Eckles, the appointee for chief justice of Utah, and took an oath; but why did he swear so recklessly when the one before whom he swore was no more an official than himself?

The army wintered at a satisfactory distance from Salt Lake City, and such a winter, according to official reports, the soldiers of our nation have rarely had to brave. It was soon apparent that they need fear no "Mormon" attack; orders had been issued to the territorial militia to take no life except in cases of absolute necessity; but General Johnston and his staff had more than their match in battling with the elements. Communications between Governor Young and the commandant were frequent; safe conduct was assured any and all officers who chose to enter the city; and if necessary hostages were to be given; but the governor was inexorable in his ultimatum that, as an organized body with hostile purpose, the soldiers should not pass the mountain gateway. In the meantime, a full account of the situation was reported by Governor Young to the President of the United States, and the truth slowly made its way into the eastern press. President Buchanan tacitly admitted his mistake; but to recall the troops at that juncture would be to confess humiliating failure.

A peace commissioner, in the person of Colonel Kane, was dispatched to Salt Lake City; his coming being made known to Governor Young, an escort was sent to meet him and conduct him through the "Mormon" lines. The result of the conference was that the "Mormon" leaders but reiterated their statement that the President's appointees would be given safe entry to the city, and be duly installed in their offices, provided they would enter without the army. This ultimatum was carried to the federal camp; and to the open chagrin of the commandant, Governor Cumming and his fellow appointees moved to Salt Lake City under "Mormon" escort, after a five months' halt in the wilderness.

I believe that strategy is usually allowed in war, and I am free to say the "Mormons" availed themselves of this license. At short intervals in the course of the night-passage through the canyon, the party was challenged, and the password demanded; bon-fires were blazing down in the gorges, and the impression was made that the mountains were full of armed men; whereas the sentries were members of the escort, who, preceding by short cuts the main party, continued to challenge and to pass. On their arrival, the gentlemen were met by the retiring officials, and were peaceably installed. The new governor called upon the clerk of the court, and ascertained the truth of the statement that the records were entirely safe. He promptly reported his conclusions to General Johnston that there was no further need for the army. It was decided, however, that the soldiers should be permitted to march through the city, and straightway the "Mormons" began their exodus to the south.

Governor Cumming tried in vain to induce the people to remain, assuring them that the troops would commit no depredations. "Not so," said Brigham Young, "we have had experience with troops in the past, Governor Cumming; we have seen our leaders shot down by the demoralized soldiery; we have seen mothers with babes at their breasts sent to their last home by the same bullet; we have witnessed outrages beyond description. You are now Governor of Utah; we can no longer command the militia for our own defense. We do not wish to fight, therefore we depart." Leaving a few men to apply the brand to the combustibles stored in every house, at the first sign of plunder by the soldiers, the people again deserted their homes and moved into the desert anew.

But the officers of the army kept their word; the troops were put into camp forty miles from the settlements, and the settlers returned. The President's commissioners brought the official pardon, unsolicited, for all acts committed by the "Mormons" in opposing the entrance of the army. The people asked what they had done that needed pardon; they had not robbed, they had not killed. But a critical analysis of these troublous events revealed at least one overt act—some "Mormon" scouts had challenged a supply train; and, being opposed, they had destroyed some of the wagons and provisions; and for this they accepted the President's most gracious pardon.

CHAPTER V

After all, the "Mormon" people regard the advent of the Buchanan army as one of the greatest material blessings ever brought to them.

The troops, once in Utah, had to be provisioned; and everything the settlers could spare was eagerly bought at an unusual price. The gold changed hands. Then, in their hasty departure, the soldiers disposed of everything outside of actual necessities in the way of accouterment and camp equipage. The army found the people in poverty, and left them in comparative wealth.

And what was the cause of this hurried departure of the military? For many months, ominous rumblings had been heard,—indications of the gathering storm which was soon to break in the awful fury of civil strife. It could not be doubted that war was imminent; already the conflict had begun, and a picked part of the army was away in the western wilds, doing nothing for any phase of the public good. But a word further concerning the expedition in general. The sending of troops to Utah was part of a foul scheme to weaken the government in its impending struggle with the secessionists. The movement has been called not inaptly "Buchanan's blunder," but the best and wisest men may make blunders, and whatever may be said of President Buchanan's short-sightedness in taking this step, even his enemies do not question his integrity in the matter. He was unjustly charged with favoring secession; but the charge was soon disproved.

However, it was known that certain of his cabinet were in league with the seceding states; and prominent among them was John Floyd, secretary of war. The successful efforts of this officer to disarm the North, while accumulating the munitions of war in the South; to scatter the forces by locating them in widely separated and remote stations; and in other ways to dispose of the regular army in the manner best calculated to favor the anticipated rebellion, are matters of history. It is also told how, at the commencement of the rebellion, he allied himself with the confederate forces, accepting the rank of brigadier-general. It was through Floyd's advice that

Buchanan ordered the military expedition to Utah, ostensibly to install certain federal officials and to repress an alleged infantile rebellion which in fact had never come into existence, but in reality to further the interests of the secessionists. When the history of that great struggle with its antecedent and its consequent circumstances is written with a pen that shall indite naught but truth, when prejudice and partisanship are lived down, it may appear that Jefferson Davis rather than James Buchanan was the prime cause of the great mistake.

And General Johnston who commanded the army in the west; he who was so vehement in his denunciation of the rebel "Mormons," and who rejoiced in being selected to chastise them into submission; who, because of his vindictiveness incurred the ill-favor of the governor, whose *posse comitatus* the army was; what became of him, at one time so popular that he was spoken of as a likely successor to Winfield Scott in the office of general-in-chief of the United States army? He left Utah in the early stages of the rebellion, turned his arms against the flag he had sworn to defend, doffed the blue, donned the grey, and fell a rebel on the field of Shiloh.

Changes many and great followed in bewildering succession in Utah. The people were besought to take sides with the South in the awful scenes of cruel strife; it was openly stated in the east that Utah had allied herself with the cause of secession; and by others that the design was to make Salt Lake City the capital of an independent government. And surely such conjectures were pardonable on the part of all whose ignorance and prejudice still nursed the delusion of "Mormon" disloyalty. Moreover, had the people been inclined to rebellion what greater opportunity could they have wished? Already a North and a South were talked of—why not set up also a West? A supreme opportunity had come and how was it used? It was at this very time that the Overland Telegraph line, which had been approaching from the Atlantic and the Pacific, was completed, and the first tremor felt in that nerve of steel carried these words from Brigham Young:

> Utah has not seceded, but is firm for the constitution and laws of our country.

The "Mormon" people saw in their terrible experiences and in the outrages to which they had been subjected, only the maladministration of laws and the subversion of justice through human incapacity and hatred. Never even for a moment did they question the supreme authority and the inspired origin of the constitution of their land. They knew no North, no South, no East, no West; they stood positively by the constitution, and would have nothing to do in the bloody strife between brothers, unless indeed they were summoned by the authority to which they had already once loyally responded, to furnish men and arms for their country's need.

Following the advent of the telegraph came the railway; and the land of "Mormondom" was no longer isolated. Her resources were developed, her wealth became a topic of the world's wonder; the tide of immigration swelled her population, contributing much of the best from all the civilized nations of the earth. Every reader of recent and current history has learned of her rapid growth; of her repeated appeals for the recognition to which she had so long been entitled in the sisterhood of states; of the prompt refusals with which her pleas were persistently met, though other territories with smaller and more illiterate populations, more restricted resources, and in every way weaker claims, were allowed to assume the habiliments of maturity, while Utah, lusty, large and strong, was kept in swaddling clothes. But the cries of the vigorous infant were at length heeded, and in answer to the seventh appeal of the kind, Utah's star was added to the nation's galaxy.

But let us turn more particularly to the history of the Church itself. For a second time and thrice thereafter, the Church of Jesus Christ of Latter-day Saints has been deprived of its president, and on each occasion were reiterated the prophecies of disruption uttered at the time of Joseph Smith's assassination. Calm observers declared that as the shepherd had gone, the flock would soon be dispersed; while others, comparable only to wolves, thinking the fold unguarded, sought to harry and scatter the sheep. But "Mormonism" died not; every added pang of grief served but to unite the people.

When Brigham Young passed from earth, he was mourned of the people as deeply as was Moses of Israel. And had he not proved himself a Moses, aye and a Joshua, too? He had led the people into the land of holy promise, and had divided unto them their inheritances. He was a man with clear title as one of the small brotherhood we call great. As carpenter, farmer, pioneer, capitalist, financier, preacher, apostle, prophet—in everything he was a leader among men. Even those who opposed him in politics and in religion respected him for his talents, his magnanimity, his liberality, and his manliness; and years after his demise, men who had refused him honor while alive brought their mites and their gold to erect a monument of stone and bronze to the memory of this man who needs it not. With his death closed another epoch in the history of his people, and a successor arose, one who was capable of leading and judging under the changed conditions.

——————

But perhaps I am suspected of having forgotten or of having intentionally omitted reference to what popular belief once considered the chief feature of "Mormonism," the cornerstone of the structure, the secret of its influence over its members, and of its attractiveness to its proselytes, viz., the peculiarity of the "Mormon" institution of marriage. The Latter-day Saints were long regarded as a polygamous people. That plural marriage has been practised by a limited proportion of the people, under sanction of Church ordinance, has never since the introduction of the system been denied. But that plural marriage is a vital tenet of the Church is not true. What the Latter-day Saints call celestial marriage is characteristic of the Church, and is in very general practise; but of celestial marriage, plurality of wives was an incident, never an essential. Yet the two have often been confused in the popular mind.

We believe in a literal resurrection and an actual hereafter, in which future state shall be recognized every sanctified and authorized relationship existing here on earth—of parent and child, brother and sister, husband and wife. We believe, further that contracts as of marriage, to be valid beyond the veil of mortality must be sanctioned by a power greater than that of earth. With the seal of the holy Priesthood upon their wedded state, these people believe implicitly in the perpetuity of that relationship on the far side of the grave. They marry not with the saddening limitation "Until death do you part," but "For time and for all eternity."[3] This constitutes celestial marriage. The thought that plural marriage has ever been the head and front of "Mormon" offending, that to it is traceable as the true cause the hatred of other sects and the unpopularity of the Church, is not tenable to the earnest thinker. Sad as have been the experiences of the people in consequence of this practise, deep and anguish-laden as have been the sighs and groans, hot and bitter as have been the tears so caused, the heaviest persecution, the cruelest treatment of their history began before plural marriage was known in the Church.

[Footnote 3: For treatment of Celestial Marraige and other Temple ordinances, see "The House of the Lord," by the present author, Salt Lake City, Utah, 1912.]

There is no sect nor people that sets a higher value on virtue and chastity than do the Latter-day Saints, nor a people that visits surer retribution upon the heads of offenders against the laws of sexual purity. To them marriage is not, can never be, a civil compact alone; its significance reaches beyond the grave; its obligations are eternal; and the Latter-day Saints are notable for the sanctity with which they invest the marital state. It has been my privilege to tread the soil of many lands, to observe the customs and study the habits of more nations than one; and I have yet to find the place and meet the people, where and with whom the purity of man and woman is held more precious than among the maligned "Mormons" in the mountain valleys of the west. There I find this measure of just equality of the sexes— *that the sins of man shall not be visited upon the head of woman*.

At the inception of plural marriage among the Latter-day Saints, there was no law, national or state, against its practise. This statement assumes, as granted, a distinction between bigamy and the "Mormon" institution of plural marriage. In 1862, a law was enacted with the purpose of suppressing plural marriage, and, as had been predicted in the national Senate prior to its passage, it lay for many years a dead letter. Federal judges and United States attorneys in Utah, who were not "Mormons" nor lovers of "Mormonism," refused to entertain complaints or prosecute cases under the law, because of its manifest injustice and inadequacy. But other laws followed, most of which, as the Latter-day Saints believe, were aimed directly at their religious conception of the marriage contract, and not at social impropriety nor sexual offense.

At last the Edmunds-Tucker act took effect, making not the marriage alone but the subsequent acknowledging of the contract an offense punishable by fine or imprisonment or both. Under the spell of unrighteous zeal, the federal judiciary of Utah announced and practised that most infamous doctrine of segregation of offenses with accumulating penalties.

I who write have listened to judges instructing grand juries in such terms as these: that although the law of Congress designated as an offense the acknowledging of more living wives than one by any man, and prescribed a penalty therefor, as Congress had not specified the length of time during which this unlawful acknowledging must continue to constitute the offense, grand juries might indict separately for every day of the period during which the forbidden relationship existed. This meant that for an alleged misdemeanor—for which Congress prescribed a maximum penalty of six months' imprisonment and a fine of three hundred dollars—a man might be imprisoned for life, aye, for many terms of a man's natural life did the court's power to enforce its sentences extend so far, and might be fined millions of dollars. Before this travesty on the administration of law could be brought before the court of last resort, and there meet with the reversal and rebuke it deserved, men were imprisoned under sentences of many years' duration.

The people contested these measures one by one in the courts; presenting in case after case the different phases of the subject, and urging the unconstitutionality of the measure. Then the Church was disincorporated, and its property both real and personal confiscated and escheated to the government of the United States; and although the personal property was soon restored, real estate of great value long lay in the hands of the court's receiver, and the "Mormon" Church had to pay the national government high rental on its own property. But the people have suspended the practise of plural marriage; and the testimony of the governors, judges, and district attorneys of the territory, and later that of the officers of the state, have declared the sincerity of the renunciation.

As the people had adopted the practise under what was believed to be divine approval, they suspended it when they were justified in so doing. In whatever light this practise has been regarded in the past, it is today a dead issue, forbidden by ecclesiastical rule as it is prohibited by legal statute. And the world is learning, to its manifest surprise, that plural marriage and "Mormonism" are not synonymous terms.

– – – – – -

And so the story of "Mormonism" runs on; its finale has not yet been written; the current press presents continuously new stages of its progress, new developments of its plan. Today the Church of Jesus Christ of Latter-day Saints is stronger than ever before; and the people are confident that it is at its weakest stage for all time to come. It lives and thrives because within it are the elements of thrift and the forces of life. It embraces a boundless liberality of belief and practise; true toleration is one of its essential features; it makes love for mankind second only to love for Deity. Its creed provides for the protection of all men in their rights of worship according to the dictates of conscience. It contemplates a millennium of peace, when every man shall love his neighbor and respect his neighbor's opinion as he regards himself and his own—a day when the voice of the people shall be in unison with the voice of God.

THE PHILOSOPHY OF "MORMONISM"

CHAPTER I

In this attempt to treat the philosophy of "Mormonism" it is assumed that no discussion of Christianity in general nor of the philosophy of Christianity is required. The "Mormon" creed, so far as there is a creed professed by the Latter-day Saints, is pre-eminently Christian in theory, precept, and practise. In what respect, then, may be properly asked, does "Mormonism" differ from the faith and practise of other professedly Christian systems—in short, what is "Mormonism?"

First, let it be remembered that the term "Mormon," with its derivatives, is not the official designation of the Church with which it is usually associated. The name was originally applied in a spirit of derision, as a nick-name in fact, by the opponents of the Church; and was doubtless suggested by the title of a prominent publication given to the world through Joseph Smith in an early period of the Church's history. This, of course, is the Book of Mormon. Nevertheless, the people have accepted the name thus thrust upon them, and answer readily to its call. The proper title of the organization is "The Church of Jesus Christ of Latter-day Saints." The philosophy of "Mormonism" is declared in the name. The people claim this name as having been bestowed by revelation and therefore that, like other names given of God as attested by scriptural instances, it is at once name and title combined.

The Church declines to sail under any flag of man-made design; it repudiates the name of mortals as a part of its title, and thus differs from Lutherans and Wesleyans, Calvinists, Mennonites, and many others, all of whom, worthy though their organizations may be, elevating as may be their precepts, good as may be their practises, declare themselves the followers of men. This is not the church of Moses nor the prophets, of Paul nor of Cephas, of Apollos nor of

John; neither of Joseph Smith nor of Brigham Young. It asserts its proud claim as the Church of Jesus Christ.

It refuses to wear a name indicative of distinctive or peculiar doctrines; and in this particular, it differs from churches Catholic and Protestant, Presbyterian, Congregationalist, Unitarian, Methodist and Baptist; its sole distinguishing features are those of the Church of Christ.

In an effort to present in concise form the cardinal doctrines of this organization, I cannot do better than quote the so-called *Articles of Faith of the Church of Jesus Christ of Latter-day Saints*, which have been in published form before the world for over half a century.[4]

[Footnote 4: For extended treatment of "Mormon" doctrine see "The Articles of Faith: a Series of Lectures on the Principal Doctrines of the Church of Jesus Christ of Latter-day Saints," by James E. Talmage. Published by the Church: Salt Lake City, Utah; 485 pp.]

1. We believe in God, the Eternal Father, and in His Son, Jesus Christ, and in the Holy Ghost.

2. We believe that men will be punished for their own sins, and not for Adam's transgression.

3. We believe that, through the atonement of Christ, all mankind may be saved, by obedience to the laws and ordinances of the gospel.

4. We believe that the first principles and ordinances of the gospel are: First, Faith in the Lord Jesus Christ; second, Repentance; third, Baptism by immersion for the remission of sins; fourth, Laying on of hands for the gift of the Holy Ghost.

5. We believe that a man must be called of God, by prophecy, and by the laying on of hands, by those who are in authority, to preach the gospel and administer in the ordinances thereof.

6. We believe in the same organization that existed in the primitive church, namely, apostles, prophets, pastors, teachers, evangelists, etc.

7. We believe in the gift of tongues, prophecy, revelation, visions, healing, interpretation of tongues, etc.

8. We believe the Bible to be the word of God, as far as it is translated correctly; we also believe the Book of Mormon to be the word of God.

9. We believe all that God has revealed, all that he does now reveal, and we believe that he will yet reveal many great and important things pertaining to the Kingdom of God.

10. We believe in the literal gathering of Israel and in the restoration of the Ten Tribes; that Zion will be built upon this [the American] continent; that Christ will reign personally upon the earth, and that the earth will be renewed and receive its paradisiacal glory.

11. We claim the privilege of worshiping Almighty God according to the dictates of our own conscience, and allow all men the same privilege, let them worship how, where, or what they may.

12. We believe in being subject to kings, presidents, rulers and magistrates, in obeying, honoring and sustaining the law.

13. We believe in being honest, true, chaste, benevolent, virtuous, and in doing good to all men; indeed we may say that we follow the admonition of Paul, We believe all things, we hope all things, we have endured many things, and hope to be able to endure all things. If there is anything virtuous, lovely, or of good report or praiseworthy, we seek after these things.—JOSEPH SMITH.

This brief summary of "Mormon" doctrine appears over the signature of Joseph Smith—the man whom the Latter-day Saints accept as the instrument in divine hands of re-establishing the Church of Christ on earth, in this the Dispensation of the Fulness of Times. Let it not be supposed, however, that these Articles of Faith are, or profess to be, a complete code of the doctrines of the Church, for, as declared in one of the "Articles," belief in continuous revelation from Heaven is a characteristic feature of "Mormonism." Yet it is to be noted that no doctrine has been promulgated, which by even strained interpretation could be construed as antagonistic to this early declaration of faith. Nor has any revelation to the Church yet appeared in opposition to earlier revelation of this or of by-gone dispensations.

To most of the declarations in the Articles of Faith, many sects professing Christianity could confidently pledge allegiance; to many of them, all Christian organizations could and professedly do subscribe. Belief in the existence and powers of the Supreme Trinity; in Jesus Christ as the Savior and Redeemer of mankind; in man's individual accountability for his doings; in the acceptance of sacred writ as the Word of God; in the rights of Worship according to the dictates of conscience; in all the moral virtues;—these professions and beliefs are as a common creed in the realm of Christendom. There is no peculiarly "Mormon" interpretation, in the light of which these principles of faith and practise are viewed by the Latter-day Saints, except in a certain simplicity and literalness of acceptance—gross literalness, unrefined materialism, it has been called by some critical opponents.

The gospel plan as accepted and taught by the Latter-day Saints is strikingly simple; disappointing in its simplicity, indeed, to the mind that can find satisfaction in mysteries alone, and to him whose love for metaphor, symbolism, and imagery are stronger than his devotion to truth itself, which may or may not be thus embellished. The Church asserts that the wisdom of human learning, while ranking among the choicest of earthly possessions, is not essential to an understanding of the gospel; and that the preacher of the Word must be otherwise endowed than by the learning of the schoolmen. "Mormonism" is for the wayfaring man, not less than for the scholar, and it possesses a simplicity adapting it to the one as to the other. A few of the characteristically "Mormon" tenets may perhaps be profitably considered.

"Mormonism" affirms its unqualified belief in the Godhead as the Holy Trinity, comprising Father, Son, and Holy Ghost; each of the three a separate and individual personage; the Father and the Son each a personage of spirit and of immortalized body; the Holy Ghost a personage of spirit.

The unity of the Godhead is accepted in the literal fulness of scriptural declaration—that the three are one in purpose, plan and method, alike in all their Godly attributes; one in their divine omniscience and omnipotence; yet as separate and distinct in their personality as are any three inhabitants of earth. "Mormonism" claims that scriptures declaring the oneness of the Trinity admit of this interpretation; that such indeed is the natural interpretation; and that the conception is in accord with reason.

We hold that mankind are literally the spiritual children of God; that even as the Christ had an existence with the Father before coming to earth to take upon himself a tabernacle of flesh, to live and to die as a man in accordance with the fore-ordained plan of redemption, so, too, every child of earth had an existence in the spirit-state before entering upon this mortal probation. We hold the doctrine to be reasonable, scriptural and true, that mortal birth is no more the beginning of the soul's existence than is death its end.

The time-span of mortal life is but one stage in the soul's career, separating the eternity that has preceded from the eternity that is to follow. And this mortal existence is one of the Father's great gifts to his spiritual children, affording them the opportunity of an untrammeled exercise of their free agency, the privilege of meeting temptation and of resisting it if they will, the chance to win exaltation and eternal life.

We claim that all men are equal as to earthly rights and human privileges; but that each has individual capacity and capabilities; that in the primeval world there were spirits noble and great, as there were others of lesser power and inferior purpose. There is no chance in the number or nature of spirits that are born to earth; all who are entitled to the privileges of mortality and have been assigned to this sphere shall come at the time appointed, and shall return to inherit each the glory or the degradation to which he has shown himself adapted. The gospel as understood by the Latter-day

Saints affirms the unconditional free-agency of man—his right to accept good or evil, to choose the means of eternal progression or the opposite, to worship as he elects, or to refuse to worship at all—and then to take the consequences of his choice.

"Mormonism" rejects what it regards as a heresy, the false doctrine of pre-destination as an absolute compulsion or even as an irresistible tendency forced upon the individual toward right or wrong—as a pre-appointment to eventual exaltation or condemnation; yet it affirms that the infinite wisdom and fore-knowledge of God makes plain to him the end from the beginning; and that he can read in the natures and dispositions of his children, their destiny.

"Mormonism" claims an actual and literal relationship of parent and child between the Creator and man—not in the figurative sense in which the engine may be called the child of its builder; not the relationship of a thing mechanically made to the maker thereof; but the kinship of father and offspring. In short it is bold enough to declare that man's spirit being the offspring of Deity, and man's body though of earthy components yet being in the very image and likeness of God, man even in his present degraded—aye, fallen condition—still possesses, if only in a latent state, inherited traits, tendencies and powers that tell of his more than royal descent; and that these may be developed so as to make him, even while mortal, in a measure Godlike.

But "Mormonism" is bolder yet. It asserts that in accordance with the inviolable law of organic nature—that like shall beget like, and that multiplication of numbers and perpetuation of species shall be in compliance with the condition "each after his kind," the child may achieve the former status of the parent, and that in his mortal condition man is a God in embryo. However far in the future it may be, what ages may elapse, what eternities may pass before any individual now a mortal being may attain the rank and sanctity of godship, man nevertheless carries in his soul the possibilities of such achievement; even as the crawling caterpillar or the corpse-like chrysalis holds the latent possibility, nay, barring destruction, the certainty indeed, of the winged imago in all the glory of maturity.

"Mormonism" claims that all nature, both on earth and in heaven, operates on a plan of advancement; that the very Eternal Father is a progressive Being; that his perfection, while so complete as to be incomprehensible by man, possesses this essential quality of true perfection—the capacity of eternal increase. That therefore, in the far future, beyond the horizon of eternities perchance, man may attain the status of a God. Yet this does not mean that he shall be then the equal of the Deity he now worships nor that he shall ever overtake those intelligences that are already beyond him in advancement; for to assert such would be to argue that there is no progression beyond a certain stage of attainment, and that advancement is a characteristic of low organization and inferior purpose alone. We believe that there was more than the sounding of brass or the tinkling of wordy cymbals in the fervent admonition of the Christ to his followers—"Be ye therefore perfect, even as your Father which is in heaven is perfect." (Matt. 5:48.)

But it is beyond dispute that in his present state, man is far from the condition of even a relatively perfect being. He is born heir to the weaknesses as well as to the excellencies of generations of ancestors; he inherits potent tendencies for both good and evil; and verily, it seems that in the flesh he has to suffer for the sins of his progenitors. But divine blessings are not to be reckoned in terms of earthly possessions or bodily excellencies alone; the child born under conditions of adversity may after all be richly endowed with opportunity, opportunity which, perhaps, had been less of service amid the surroundings of luxury. We hold that the Father has an individual interest in his children; and that surely in the rendering of divine judgment, the conditions under which each soul has lived in mortality shall be considered.

"Mormonism" accepts the doctrine of the Fall, and the account of the transgression in Eden, as set forth in Genesis; but it affirms that none but Adam is or shall be answerable for Adam's disobedience; that mankind in general are absolutely absolved from responsibility for that "original sin," and that each shall account for his own transgressions alone; that the Fall was foreknown of God—that it was turned to good effect by which the necessary condition of mortality should be inaugurated; and that a Redeemer was provided, before the world was; that general salvation, in the sense of redemption from the effects of the Fall, comes to all without their seeking it; but that individual salvation or rescue from the effects of personal sins is to be acquired by each for himself by faith and good works through the redemption wrought by Jesus Christ. The Church holds that children are born to earth in a sinless state, that they need no individual redemption; that should they die before reaching years of accountability, they return without taint of earthly sin; but as they attain youth or maturity in the flesh, their responsibility increases with their development.

According to the teachings of "Mormonism," Christ's instructions to the people to pray "Thy Kingdom come, thy will be done, on earth as it is in heaven" was not a petition for the impossible, but a fore-shadowing of what shall eventually be. We believe that the day shall yet come when the Kingdom of God on earth shall be one with the Kingdom in heaven; and one King shall rule in both. The Church is regarded as the beginning of this Kingdom on earth; though until the coming of the King, there is no authority in the Church exercising or claiming temporal rule or dominion among the governments of earth. Yet the Church is none the less the beginning of the Kingdom, the germ from which the Kingdom shall develop.

And the Church must be in direct communication with the heavenly Kingdom of which the earthly Kingdom when established shall be a part. Of such a nature was the Church in so far as it existed before the time of Christ's earthly ministry; for the biblical record is replete with instances of direct communication between the prophets and their God. The scriptures are silent as to a single dispensation in which the spiritual leaders of the people depended upon the records of earlier times and by-gone ages for their guidance; but on the contrary, the evidence is complete that in every stage of the Church's history the God of heaven communicated his mind and will unto his earthly representatives. Israel of old were led and governed in all matters spiritual and to a great extent in their temporal affairs by the direct word of revelation. Noah did not depend upon the record of God's dealings with Adam or Enoch, but was directed by the very word and voice of the God whom he represented. Moses was no mere theologian trained for his authority or acts on what God had said to Abraham, to Isaac, or to Jacob; he acted in accordance with instructions given unto him from time to time, as the circumstances of his ministry required. And so on through all the line of prophets, major and minor, down to the priest of the course of Abia unto whom the angel announced the birth of John who was to be the direct fore-runner of the Messiah.

When the Christ came in the flesh he declared that he acted not of himself but according to instructions given him of the Father. Thus the Messiah was a revelator, receiving while in the flesh communication direct and frequent from the heavens. By such revelation he was guided in his earthly ministry; by such he instructed his disciples; unto such he taught his apostles to look for safe guidance when he would have left them.

During his earthly ministry Christ called and ordained men to offices in the Church. We have a record of apostles particularly, numbering twelve, and beside these, seventy others who were commissioned to preach, teach, baptize and perform other ordinances of the Church. After our Lord's departure, we read of the apostles continuing their labors in the light of continued revelation. By this sure guide they selected and set apart those who were to officiate in the Church. By revelation, Peter was directed to carry the gospel to the Gentiles; which expansion of the work was inaugurated by the conversion of the devout Cornelius and his household. By revelation, Saul of Tarsus became Paul the Apostle, a valiant defender of the faith. Holy men of old spake and wrote as they were moved upon by the Holy Ghost and depended not upon the precedents of ancient history nor entirely upon the law then already written. They operated under the conviction that the living Church must be in communication with its living Head; and that the work of God, while it was to be wrought out through the instrumentality of man, was to be directed by him whose work it was, and is.

"Mormonism" claims the same necessity to exist today. It holds that it is no more nearly possible now than it was in the days of the ancient prophets or in the apostolic age for the Church of Christ to exist without direct and continuous revelation from God. This necessitates the existence and authorized ministrations of prophets, apostles, high priests, seventies, elders, bishops, priests, teachers and deacons, now as anciently—not men selected by men without authority, clothed by human ceremonial alone, nor men with the empty names of office, but men who bear the title because they possess the authority, having been called of God.

Is it unreasonable, is it unphilosophical, thus to look for additional light and knowledge? Shall religion be the one department of human thought and effort in which progression is impossible? What would we say of the chemist, the astronomer, the physicist, or the geologist, who would proclaim that no further discovery or revelation of scientific truth is possible, or who would declare that the only occupation open to students of science is to con the books of by-gone times and to apply the principles long ago made known, since none others shall ever be discovered?

The chief motive impelling to research and investigation is the conviction that to knowledge and wisdom there is no end. "Mormonism" affirms that all wisdom is of God, that the halo of his glory is intelligence, and that man has not yet learned all there is to learn of him and his ways. We hold that the doctrine of continuous revelation from God is not less philosophical and scientific than scriptural.

CHAPTER II

The Latter-day Saints affirm that the authority to act in the name of God—the Holy Priesthood—has been restored to earth in this dispensation and age, in accordance with the inspired predictions of earlier times. But, it may be asked, what necessity was there for a restoration if the Priesthood had been once established upon earth? None indeed, had it never been taken away. A general apostasy from the primitive Church is conceded in effect by some authorities in ecclesiastical history; though few admit the entire discontinuance of priestly power, or the full suspension of authority to operate in the ordinances of the Church. This great apostasy was foretold. Paul warned the Saints of Thessalonica against those who claimed that the second coming of Christ was then near at hand: "For," said he, "that day shall not come except there come a falling away first." (II Thess. 2:3.) "Mormonism" contends that there has been a general falling away from the Church of Christ, dating from the time immediately following the apostolic period. We believe that the proper interpretation of history will confirm this view; and, moreover, that the inspired scriptures foretold just such a condition.[5]

[Footnote 5: See "The Great Apostasy: Considered in the Light of Scriptural and Secular History," by James E. Talmage. Published by the *Deseret News*, Salt Lake City, Utah; 176 pp.]

If the Priesthood had been once taken from the earth no human power could re-establish it; the restoration of this authority from heaven would be necessary. The Church claims that in the present age this restoration has been effected by the personal ministrations of those who exercised the authority in earlier dispensations. Thus, in 1829, Joseph Smith and Oliver Cowdery received the Lesser or Aaronic Priesthood under the hands of John the Baptist, who visited them as a resurrected being—the same Baptist who by special and divine commission held the authority of that Priesthood in the dispensation of the "Meridian of Time." Later, the Higher or Melchizedek Priesthood was conferred upon them through the personal ministrations of Peter, James, and John—the same three who constituted the presidency of the apostolic body in the primitive Church, after the departure of the Lord Jesus Christ by whom it was founded.

That the claim is a bold one is conceded without argument. The Church of Jesus Christ of Latter-day Saints professes to have the Priesthood of old restored in its fulness; and, moreover, while acknowledging the right of every individual as of every sect or other organization of individuals to believe and practise according to choice in matters religious, it affirms that it is the only Church on the face of the earth possessing this authority and Priesthood; and that therefore it is *The Church* and the only Church of Christ upon the earth today. It holds as absolutely indispensable to proper Church organization, the presence of the living oracles of God who shall be directed from the heavens in their earthly ministry; and these, "Mormonism" asserts, are to be found with the Church of Jesus Christ.

"Mormonism" emphasizes the doctrine that that which is Caesar's be given unto Caesar, while that which is God's be rendered unto him. Therefore, it teaches that all things pertaining unto earth, and unto man's earthly affairs, may with propriety be regulated by earthly authority, but that in the performance of any ordinance, rite, or ceremony, claimed to be of effect beyond, the grave, a power greater than that of man is requisite or the performance is void. Therefore, membership in the Church, which, if of any value and significance at all, is of more than temporal meaning, must be governed by laws which are prescribed by the powers of heaven. "Mormonism" recognizes Jesus Christ as the head of the Church, as the literal Savior and Redeemer of mankind, as the King of kings and Lord of lords, as the One whose right it is to reign on earth, who shall yet subdue all worldly kingdoms under his feet, who shall present the earth in its final state of redemption to the Father. It is his right to prescribe the conditions under which mankind may be made partakers of his bounty and of the privileges of the victory won by him over death and the grave.

The Church claims that faith in God is essential to intelligent service of him; and that faith, trust, confidence in God as the Father of mankind, as the Supreme Being to whom all shall render account of their deeds and misdeeds, must lead to a desire to serve him and thus produce repentance. Faith in God and genuine repentance of sin, of necessity, therefore constitute the fundamental principles of the gospel. It is reasonable to expect that after man has developed faith in God, and has repented of his sins, he will be eager to find a means of demonstrating his sincerity; and this means is found in the requirement concerning baptism as essential to entrance into the Church, and as a means whereby remission of sins may be obtained. As to the mode of baptism, the Church affirms that immersion alone is the one method sanctioned by scripture, and that this mode has been expressly prescribed by revelation in the present dispensation.

Water baptism, then, becomes a basic principle and the first essential ordinance of the gospel. It is to be administered by one having authority; and that authority rests in the Priesthood given of God. Following baptism by water, comes the ordinance of the bestowal of the Holy Ghost by the authorized imposition of hands, which constitutes the true baptism of the Spirit. These requirements, designated specifically the "first principles and ordinances of the gospel," "Mormonism" claims to be absolutely essential to membership in the Church of Christ, and this without modification or qualification as to the time at which the individual lived in mortality.

Then with propriety it may be asked:—What shall become of those who lived and died while the Priesthood was not operative upon the earth?—those who have worked out their mortal probation during the ages of the great apostasy? Furthermore, what shall be the destiny of those who, though living in a time of spiritual light, perhaps had not the opportunity of learning and obeying the gospel requirements? Here again the inherent justice of "Mormon" philosophy shows itself in the doctrine of salvation for the dead. No distinction is made between the living and the dead in the solemn declaration of the Savior to Nicodemus, which appears to have been given the widest possible application,—that except a man be born of water and of the spirit he cannot enter into the Kingdom of God. (John 3:1-5.)

"Mormonism" proclaims something more than a heaven and a hell, to one or the other of which all spirits of men shall be assigned, perhaps on the basis of a very narrow margin of merit or demerit. As it affirms the existence of an infinite range of graded intelligences, so it claims the widest and fullest gradation of conditions of future existence. It holds that the honest, though, perchance, mistaken soul who lived or tried to live according to the light he had received, shall be counted among the honorable of the earth, and shall find opportunity, if not here then in the hereafter, for compliance with the requirements essential for salvation. It teaches that repentance with all its attendant blessings shall be possible beyond the grave; but that inasmuch as the change we call death does not transform the character of the soul, repentance there will be difficult for him who has ruthlessly and willfully rejected the manifold opportunities afforded him for repentance here. It asserts that even the heathen devotee who may have bowed down to stocks and stones, if in so doing he was obeying the highest law of worship which to his benighted soul had come, shall have part in the first resurrection, and shall be afforded the opportunity, which on earth he had not found, of doing that which is required of God's children for salvation. And for all the dead who have been without the privileges, perhaps indeed without the knowledge, of compliance with Christ's law, there shall be given opportunity in the hereafter.

Nevertheless, this life of ours is no trifle, no insignificant incident in the soul's eternal course, having but small and temporal importance, the omissions of which can be rectified with ease by the individual beyond the veil. If compliance with the divine law as exemplified by the requirements of faith, repentance, baptism, and the bestowal of the right to the ministrations of the Holy Ghost, are essential to the salvation of those few who just now are counted among the living, such is not less necessary for those who once were living but now are dead. Who are the living of today but those who shortly shall be added to the uncounted dead? Who are the dead but those who at some time have lived in mortality?

Christ has been ordained to be judge of both quick and dead; he is Lord of living and dead as man uses these terms, for all live unto him. How then shall the dead receive the blessings and ordinances denied to them or by them neglected while in the flesh? "Mormonism" answers: By the vicarious work of the living in their behalf! It was this great and privileged labor to which the prophet Malachi referred in his solemn declaration, that before the great and dreadful day of the Lord, Elijah should be sent with the commission to turn the hearts of the fathers to the children and the hearts of the children to the fathers. Elijah's visitation to earth has been realized. On the 3rd of April, in the year 1836, there appeared unto Joseph Smith and Oliver Cowdery, in the temple erected by the. Latter-day Saints at Kirtland, Ohio, Elijah the prophet, who announced that the time spoken of by Malachi had fully come; then and there he bestowed the authority, for this dispensation, to inaugurate and carry on this labor in behalf of the departed.

As to the fidelity with which the Latter-day Saints have sought to discharge the duties thus divinely required at their hands, let the temples erected in poverty as in relative prosperity—by the blood and tears of the people—testify. Two of these great edifices were constructed by the Latter-day Saints in the days of their tribulation, in times of their direst persecution,—one at Kirtland, Ohio, the other at Nauvoo, Illinois. The first is still standing, though no longer possessed by the people who built it; and no longer employed for the furtherance of the purposes of its erection; the second fell a prey to flames enkindled by mobocratic hate. Four others have been constructed in the vales of Utah, and are today in service, dedicated to the blessing of the living, and particularly to the vicarious labor of the living in behalf of the dead. In them the ordinances of baptism, and the laying on of hands for the bestowal of the Holy Ghost, are performed upon the living representatives of the dead.[6]

[Footnote 6: For a detailed treatment of Temples and Temple labor among the Latter-day Saints, including a study of the doctrine of vicarious labor for the dead, see "The House of the Lord, a Study of Holy Sanctuaries Ancient and Modern," including forty-six plates illustrative of modern Temples; by James E. Talmage. Published by the Church: Salt Lake City, Utah; 336 pp.]

But this labor for the dead is two-fold; it comprises the proper performance of the required ordinances on earth, and the preaching of the gospel to the departed. Shall we suppose that all of God's good gifts to his children are restricted to the narrow limits of mortal existence? We are told of the inauguration of this great missionary labor in the spirit world, as effected by the Christ himself. After his resurrection, and immediately following the period during which his body had lain in the tomb guarded by the soldiery, he declared to the sorrowing Magdalene that he had not at that time ascended to his Father; and, in the light of his dying promise to the penitent malefactor who suffered on a cross by his side, we learn that he had been in paradise. Peter also tells us of his labors—that he was preaching to the spirits in prison, to those who had been disobedient in the days of Noah when the long-suffering of God waited while the ark was preparing. If it was deemed necessary or just that the gospel be carried to spirits that were disobedient or neglectful in the days of Noah, are we justified in concluding that others who have rejected or neglected the word of God shall be left in a state of perpetual condemnation?

"Mormonism" claims that not only shall the gospel be carried to the living, and be preached to every creature, but that the great missionary labor, the burden of which has been placed on the Church, must of necessity be extended to the realm of the dead. It declares unequivocally that without compliance with the requirements established by Jesus Christ, no soul can be saved from the fate of the condemned; but that opportunity shall be given to every one in the season of his fitness to receive it, be he heathen or civilized, living or dead.

The whole duty of man is to live and work according to the highest laws of right made known to him, to walk according to the best light that has been shed about his path; and while Justice shall deny to every soul that has not rendered obedience to the law, entrance into the kingdom of the blessed, Mercy shall claim opportunity for all who, have shown themselves willing to receive the truth and obey its behests.

It will be seen, then, that "Mormonism" offers no modified or conditional claims as to the necessity of compliance with the laws and ordinances of the gospel by every responsible inhabitant of earth unto whom salvation shall come. It distinguishes not between enlightened and heathen nations, nor between men of high and low intelligence; nor even between the living and the dead. No human being who has attained years of accountability in the flesh, may hope for salvation in the kingdom of God until he has rendered obedience to the requirements of Christ, the Redeemer of the world.

But while thus decisive, "Mormonism" is not exclusive. It does not claim that all who have failed to accept and obey the gospel of eternal life shall be eternally and forever damned. While boldly asserting that the Church of Jesus Christ of Latter-day Saints is the sole repository of the Holy Priesthood as now restored to earth, it teaches and demands the fullest toleration for all individuals, and organizations of individuals, professing righteousness; and holds that each shall be rewarded for the measure of good he has wrought, to be adjudged in accordance with the spiritual knowledge he has gained. For such high claims combined with such professions of tolerance, the Church has been accused of inconsistency. Let it not be forgotten, however, that toleration is not acceptance. I may believe with the utmost fulness of my soul's powers that I am right and my neighbor is wrong concerning any proposition or principle; but such conviction gives me no semblance of right for interfering with his exercise of freedom. The only bounds to the liberty of an individual are such as mark the liberty of another, or the rights of the community. God himself treats as sacred, and therefore as inviolable, the freedom of the human soul.

"Know this, that every soul is free
To choose his life and what he'll be;
For this eternal truth is given,
That God will force no man to heaven.

"He'll call, persuade, direct aright,
Bless him with wisdom, love, and light;
In nameless ways be good and kind,
But never force the human mind."

"Mormonism" contends that no man or nation possesses the right to forcibly deprive even the heathen of his right to worship his deity. Though idolatry has been marked from the earliest ages with the seal of divine disfavor, it may represent in the unenlightened soul the sincerest reverence of which the person is capable. He should be taught better, but not compelled to render worship which to him is false because in violation of his conscience.

In further defense of the Latter-day Saints against the charge of inconsistency for this their tolerance toward others whom they verily believe to be wrong, let me again urge the cardinal principle that every man is accountable for his acts, and shall be judged in the light of the law as made known to him.

There is no claim of universal forgiveness; no unwarranted glorification of Mercy to the degrading or neglect of Justice; no thought that a single sin of omission or of commission shall fail to leave its wound or scar. In the great future there shall be found a place for every soul, whatever his grade of spiritual intelligence may be. "In my Father's house are many mansions," (John 14:2), declared the Savior to his apostles; and Paul adds, "There are also celestial bodies, and bodies terrestrial; but the glory of the celestial is one, and the glory of the terrestrial is another. There is one glory of the sun and another glory of the moon and another glory of the stars; for one star differeth from another star in glory. So also is the resurrection of the dead," (I Cor. 15:40-42). The Latter-day Saints claim a revelation of the present dispensation as supplementing the scripture just quoted. From this later scripture (see D&C, Sec. 76), we learn that there are three well-defined degrees in the future state, with numerous, perhaps numberless, gradations.

There is the *celestial state* provided for those who have lived the whole law, who have accepted the testimony of the Christ, who have complied with the required ordinances of the gospel, who have been valiant in the cause of virtue and truth. Then there is the *terrestrial state*, comparable to the first as is the moon to the sun. This shall be given to the less valiant, to many who are nevertheless among the worthy men of the earth, but who perchance have been deceived as to the gospel and its requirements. The *telestial state* is for those who have failed to live according to the light given them; those who have had to suffer the results of their sins; those who have been of Moses, of Paul, of Apollos, and of any one of a multitude of others, but not of the Christ.

We hold that there is a wide difference between salvation and exaltation; that there are infinite gradations beyond the grave as there are here, and as there were in the state preceding this.

"Mormonism" is frequently spoken of as a new religion, and the Church as a new church, a mere addition of one to the many sects that have so long striven for recognition and ascendency among men. It is new only as the springtime following the darkness and the cold of the year's night is new. The Church is a new one only as the ripening fruit is a new development in the course of the tree's growth. In a general and true sense, "Mormonism" is not new to the world. It is founded on the gospel of Christ which antedates this earth. The establishment of the Church in the present age was but a restoration. True, the Church is progressive as it ever has been; it is therefore productive of more and greater things as the years link themselves into the centuries; but the living seed contains within its husk all the possibilities of the mature plant.

This so-called new, modern gospel is in fact the old one, the first one, come again. It demands the organization and the authority characteristic of the Church in former days, when there was a Church of God upon the earth; it expects no more consideration, and scarcely hopes for greater popularity, than were accorded the primitive Church. Opposition, persecution, and martyrdom have been its portion, but these tribulations it accepts, knowing well that to bear such has been the lot of the true Church in every age.

"Mormonism" is more than a code of morals; it claims a higher rank than that of an organization of men planned and instituted by the wisdom and philosophy of men, however worthy. It draws a distinction between morality and religion; and affirms that human duty is not comprised in a mere avoidance of sin. It regards the strictest morality as an indispensable feature of every religious system claiming in any degree divine recognition; and yet it looks upon morality as but the alphabet from which the words and sentences of a truly religious life may be framed. However euphonious the words, however eloquent the periods, to make the writing of highest worth there must be present the divine thought; and this, man of himself cannot conceive.

It affirms that there was a yesterday as there is a today, and shall be a tomorrow, in the dealings of God with men; that

Through the ages one increasing purpose runs;

and that purpose,—the working out of a divine plan, the ultimate object of which is the salvation and exaltation of the human family.

The central feature of that plan was the earthly ministry and redeeming sacrifice of the Christ in the meridian of time; the consummation shall be ushered in by the return of that same Christ to earth as the Rewarder of righteousness, the Avenger of iniquity, and as the world's Judge.

The Church holds that in the light of revelation, ancient and modern, and by a fair interpretation of the signs of the times, the second coming of the Redeemer is near at hand. The present is the final dispensation of the earth in its present state; these are the last days of which the prophets in all ages have sung.

But of what use are theories and philosophies of religion without practical application? Of what avail is belief as a mere mental assent or denial? Let it develop into virile faith; vitalize it; animate it; then it becomes a moving power. The Latter-day Saints point with some confidence to what they have attempted and begun, and to the little they have already done in the line of their convictions, as proof of their sincerity.

For the second coming of the Redeemer, preparation is demanded of men; and today, instead of the single priest crying in the wilderness of Judaea, there are thousands going forth among the nations with a message as definite and as important as that of the Baptist; and their proclamation is a reiteration of the voice in the desert—"Repent Repent! for the Kingdom of Heaven is at hand."

The philosophy of "Mormonism" rests on the literal acceptance of a living, personal God, and on the unreserved compliance with his law as from time to time revealed.